MELLEN STUDIES IN LITERATURE
STUDIES IN ENGLISH
LITERATURE/ROMANTIC REASSESSMENT

"A THOUSAND IMAGES OF LOVELINESS"
in
PERCY BYSSHE SHELLEY'S LOVE POETRY

INGRID R. KITZBERGER

The Edwin Mellen Press
Lewiston•Queenston•Lampeter

ISBN 0-7734-0321-3

The Edwin Mellen Press
Box 450
Lewiston, New York
USA 14092-0450

The Edwin Mellen Press
Box 67
Queenston, Ontario
CANADA L0S 1L0

The Edwin Mellen Press, Ltd.
Lampeter, Ceredigion, Wales
UNITED KINGDOM SA48 8LT

Printed in the United States of America

Meinen Eltern

Like ocean, which the general north wind breaks
Into ten thousand waves, and each one makes
A mirror of the moon - like some great glass,
Which did distort whatever form might pass,
Dashed into fragments by a playful child,
Which then reflects its eyes and forehead mild;
Giving for one, which it could ne'er express,
A thousand images of loveliness.

Fr. Epips. 19-26

iii

ABBREVIATIONS

Const. Sing.   To Constantia, Singing
Epips.   Epipsychidion
Eug. Hills   The Euganean Hills
Fr. Epips.   Fragments Connected With Epipsychidion
Hymn Intell.   Hymn to Intellectual Beauty
Jane, Invit.   To Jane: The Invitation
Jane, Recoll.   To Jane: The Recollection
Magn. Lady   The Magnetic Lady to her Patient
Prom. Unb.   Prometheus Unbound
Revolt   The Revolt of Islam (Laon and Cythna)
Rosal.   Rosalind and Helen
Sensit. Plant   The Sensitive Plant
Zucca   The Zucca

CONTENTS

INTRODUCTION

Percy B. Shelley may rightly be called a poet and advocate of love. Indeed, the theme of love is present in all his longer and in many of his shorter poems.

Love as a noun is to be found 530 times in Shelley's total poetical work; the verb 'to love' occurs 91 times, its past tense form 75 times, and besides that there is a vast number of derivatives and composites.[1]

Shelley celebrated love as the ruling principle of an ideal universe, as the One from which all positive elements of life derive their existence and to which the world's diversity tends and in which it will once be overcome, when "to love and live be one" (Epips. 551). It is the identification of love with life to which Shelley's concept of love tends. The deficiency of the present empirical world springs from its lack of love. Therefore, the envisioned world of the future, the millennium, is a world transfigured by love.

Love, according to Shelley, is a trinity comprising three aspects: love between the sexes, love for mankind, and love for nature. In his poetry Shelley is concerned with all three, although it is not always easy to keep them apart, as one aspect is closely linked with the other.[2] Thus, Laon and Cythna in "The

---

[1] Cf. Ellis, F. S.: *A Lexical Concordance to the Poetical Works of Percy Bysshe Shelley.* London 1892, p. 417ff. - e.g. lover(s), loves; love-adept, love-child, love-devoted, love-dreams, love-enkindled, love-laden, love-lament, love-sick, love-wakening, loveless, lovely, loveliness.

[2] Cf. Leyda, Seraphia D.: *"The Serpent is Shut Out from Paradise": A Revaluation of Romantic Love in Shelley* (= *Romantic Reassessment* 4) Salzburg 1972, p. 13: "in all his work there is the basic assumption of the inseparability of the three kinds of love."

Revolt of Islam" expand their mutual love to love for all mankind
and nature; the poet's love in "Epipsychidion" shifts from nature,
the first object, to Emily, the final aim and haven of his desire.

Nevertheless, in this study emphasis is laid on love between
the sexes, as far as it could be extracted from the remaining two
aspects.

Many critics have already dealt with Shelley's concept of
love or his imagery in general, but - as far as it is known to me -
none of them has made the imagery as it appears in Shelley's love
poetry the object of his examination. I, therefore, consider the
original contribution of this investigation to be its concentration
on and detailed analysis of the imagery Shelley applies throughout
his love poetry.

Clarification and corroboration is achieved by reference to
his letters and especially to his prose work. But the primal in-
terest lies in what the poems themselves have to say, and secondary
sources - to which Shelley's prose work also belongs, if we consider it in relation to his poetry - were always used as such.

In undertaking an investigation in the large field of imagery
in Shelley's love poetry, it was necessary to select from the variety and vast number of Shelley's poems dealing with love. "The
Revolt of Islam" or "Laon and Cythna" (its original title) and
"Epipsychidion" were taken as the basis for this study.

Both poems seemed interesting to deal with, especially as the
first stems from Shelley's early period when he was still in Eng-
land; the other one is the outcome of his "Italian Platonics",
composed one and a half years before his death in July, 1822.

Nevertheless, the minor and short love poems have not been
neglected, and throughout this work special reference is made to
them; they range from the early poems dedicated to Harriet and
Mary to those he addressed to the woman who brightened up his last

year, Jane Williams.

It was my purpose to allow Shelley to speak through his poetry and especially through the imagery applied in it.[3]

For a clear definition of the exact object of this analysis, the terms 'image' and 'imagery' had to be differentiated from the terms 'symbol' and 'metaphor', which bear nearly the same meaning but nevertheless differ in their true shades of significance. Whereas the latter two are restricted to a single expression or phrase, the term 'imagery' refers to the creation of an atmosphere, a whole picture, brought about by the apprehension of reality through different senses, while simultaneously enrichening the actual scene by revealing its underlying significance.[4] This is often achieved

---

[3]Cf. Freydorf, Roswith von: *Die bildhafte Sprache in Shelley's Lyrik*. Quakenbrück 1935, p. 2: "Stilforschung ... wird immer abhängig bleiben müssen von der Fähigkeit des Forschers, sich einfühlen zu können und vor allem sich einfühlen zu wollen, von seinem ernsthaften Bemühen, sich selbst zurückzustellen und der Sprache des 'Anderen' zu lauschen."

[4]Cf. Furbank, Philip N.: *Reflections on the Word 'Image'*. London 1970, p. 1: "... the natural sense of the word 'image', as meaning a likeness, a picture, or a simulacrum... the word 'image', unlike 'metaphor', seems to suggest that the end result of what the author is doing is a picture." - cf. Freydorf, *Bildhafte Sprache* 7f.: "Bildhafte Sprache deutet nie auf ein Einzelnes, meint immer eine Vielheit, ein Mehr, als prosaische Sprache es auszudrücken imstande wäre. Sie ist eine durchsichtige Sprache, die durch sich selbst in einen hinter ihr liegenden Tiefenraum weist. Bildhafte Sprache erteilt einem einzelnen Worte oder Ausdruck Symbolfunktion, sie verneint dieses Wort, das sie immerhin als ein einzelnes und positives hingestellt hat - doch durch sich selbst wieder in seiner festen Positivität, löst sich aus ihr selbst heraus und geht in ein Vielfaches über. Sie macht das einzeln hingestellte Wort also zu einem Träger für Mannigfaltiges." - against Fogle's definition - cf. Fogle, Richard Harter: *The Imagery of Keats and Shelley. A Comparative Study*. Chapel Hill 1949, p. 20: "An image may be a single word and thus correspond to what is usually called a metaphor. It may be an explicit comparison with the two terms sympathetically linked - a simile. It may be personification, a sub-species of

4

by combining hitherto singular facts and experiences and marking
"the before unapprehended relations of things."[5]   Therein lies the
genuine power of any poet, especially one dealing with this remote
and mysterious feeling which we call love.

The imagery Shelley used in his poetry is the outcome of the
mode in which he perceived his surroundings - nature and fellow-man
alike.[6]

A poet like Shelley experiences a correspondence between nature as it affects his imagination and his own active poetic imagi-

----

[4] (cont'd) metaphor: the attribution of human thoughts and
qualities to inanimate objects, or the embodiment of abstract conceptions or state of mind in inanimate forms.   It may, in fact, be
any verbal figure of speech." - of Fogle's distinction between simple and complex imagery, the latter comes closer to the genuine
meaning of imagery - cf. p. 22: "The simple image, then, is a verbal comparison, a figure of speech.   A complex image may be a fusion of simple images, a poem, a scene from a play, or even the play
itself; it may be a recurring theme with a symbolic significance,
like a Wagnerian leitmotif."

[5] Clark, David Lee: *Shelley's Prose. Or: The Trumpet of a
Prophecy*. Albuquerque 1954, p. 278; - cf. Wright, John W.: *Shelley's Myth of Metaphor*. Athens- Georgia 1970, p. 24: "Metaphors
consist of relations synthesized by imagination from the elements of
experience."

[6] Cf. Clark, *Prose* 295: "All things exist as they are perceived
- at least in relation to the percipient." - cf. Shelley's letter to
Godwin, Dec. 11, 1817; Jones, Frederick L. (ed.): *The Letters of
Percy Bysshe Shelley*. Vol. I.II. Oxford 1964, I.577: "I am formed,
- if for anything not in common with the herd of mankind, to appre-
hend minute and remote distinctions of feeling, whether relative to
external nature of the living beings which surround us, and, to com-
municate the conceptions which result from considering either the
moral or the material universe as a whole." - cf. further his letter
to Claire Claremont, Jan. 16, 1821; Letters II, 601: "The wind,
the light, the air, the smell of a flower affects me with violent
emotions." - cf. what Wright considers to be the function of a metaphor: "metaphor is a direct instrument and form of human knowledge
- it is the mode of apprehension and expression by which imagination
creates experience." - Wright, *Myth* 11f.

nation projected into the world surrounding him.   Thus, the images applied in Shelley's poetry are partly already there to observe but are also - to some extent - a manifestation of the poetic imagination under which familiar things do not seem to be familiar any longer but it is "une nouvelle presentation de la realitê"[7], "the very image of life expressed in its eternal truth."[8]

In a letter to Peacock, Shelley once stated, "You know I always seek in what I see the manifestation of something beyond the present & tangible object."[9]

Although "the deep truth is imageless" (Prom. Unb. II.IV. 116), "Shelley's way was not to explain truth but to express it in his own particular symbolical language, to be understood by those only whose perceptions were equal to it."[10]

Thus, by using images he wanted to draw nearer to truth, and although he considered them the only and therefore necessary means[11], he was always aware that truth itself, the "white radiance of Eternity" (Adonais, LII.463), cannot be rendered by colourful images of the temporal world.

---

[7]Spurgeon, Caroline F. E.: "De L'Emploe du Symbole dans la Poesie de Shelley": *Revue Germanique* 8 (1912) 426-432, p. 428.

[8]Clark, *Prose* 281; cf. also p. 295: "it (i.e. poetry) strips the veil of familiarity from the world and lays bare the naked and sleeping beauty which is the spirit of its forms."

[9]Nov. 6, 1818; *Letters* II. 47; cf. Fogle, *Imagery* 46: "The insatiable eye of Shelley seeks always to pierce through, to go beyond physical possibility into the realm of the supernatural." - cf. Keith, Arthur L.: "The Imagery of Shelley": *South Atlantic Quarterly* 1924, 61-72, p. 61: "He refused to accept things as they seemed and was always searching for the invisible meaning."

[10]Rogers, Neville: *Shelley at Work. A Critical Inquiry.* Oxford 1956, p. 18.

[11]Cf. Butter, Peter: *Shelley's Idols of the Cave.* Edinburgh 1954, p. 33: "It seems, in fact, that images are affirmed only as a means to an end, where they shall be denied."

Shelley's realization of the insufficiency of images becomes most apparent in his love poetry, where he has to confess:

> The wingèd words on which my soul would pierce
> Into the height of Love's rare Universe,
> Are chains of lead around its flight of fire-
>
> Epips. 588-90

And again:

> There is a Power, a Love, a Joy, a God
> Which makes in mortal hearts its brief abode,
> A Pythian exhalation, which inspires
> Love, only love - a wind which o'er the wires
> Of the soul's giant harp
> There is a mood which language faints beneath.
>
> Fr. Epips. 134-39

Also in "Adonais" he reaches the conviction that

> ... words are weak
> The glory they transfuse with fitting truth to speak.
>
> Adonais, LII. 467-68

Moreover, images are insufficient from a second point of view also. Rogers found out that, "if Shelley's poetry is often difficult to read this is frequently for the reason, not least, that it was most difficult to write."[12]

"When composition begins", as Shelley himself explains this difficulty in his "Defence of Poetry", "inspiration is already on the decline, and the most glorious poetry that has ever been communicated to the world is probably a feeble shadow of the original conception of the poet"[13], and to Trelawny he once offered his solution to this problem, "When my brain gets heated with thought, it soon boils, and throws off images and words faster than I can skim

---

[12]Rogers, *Shelley* 119.

[13]Clark, *Prose* 294; for the inadequacy of language to express the poetic vision of unity and transcendence see Rosenfelt, Deborah Silverton: *Keats and Shelley: A Comparative Study of Their Ideas about Poetic Language and Some Patterns of Language Use in Their Poetry:* DA 33 (1973) 3669A.

them off.   In the morning, when cooled down, out of the rude
sketch, as you justly call it, I shall attempt a drawing."[14]

Yet the fact remains that the images occurring in the drawing
are but the shadows of the original ones.   Nevertheless, it is by
these shadows only that we can trace the poet's experience - and
this is the purpose of my examination.

In studying Shelley's images it will soon be noticed that he
applied not only visual, but also aural, tactual, kinetic (or 'kines-
thetic') images, as well as those of taste and smell.   Visual,
aural, and kinetic images range first in abundance.

Recurrent images are apparent throughout the wide range of
his love poems, though some of them occur more frequently in one
period than in the others and in different contexts.[15]

Thus, two alternatives of method lay before me when starting
this analysis: either to trace one single image, or to arrange the
images according to subjects.   As the first method is in danger of
turning into a mere dissection, spoiling the value and beauty of the
poem in question, I decided to take up the second alternative for
the sake of clarity and adequacy.

But, no doubt, the dialectic between part, i.e. a single image,
and the whole, i.e. the context in which it is placed, remains,
because "part and whole being interdependent, the full meaning of
the part is contingent on its role in the totality, but the nature

---

[14]See Rogers, *Shelley* 4.

[15]Cf. Butter, *Idols* 3: "His favourite images constitute a
symbolic shorthand language for expressing ideas as well as feel-
ings." - cf. also Freydorf, *Bildhafte Sprache* 5: "Aus elementarem
Urerlebnis steigt dem Dichter ein Bild auf und - ist es einmal
geboren worden - so kehrt es immer wieder, in seinem Bedeutungs-
gehalt, in seiner Stimmungsfarbe sich variierend, je nach seiner
Eingliederung in das Gesamterleben ... Mehr und mehr aber werden sie
zum ganz besonderen Worteigentum ihres Schöpfers."

and significance of the totality are functions of its parts."[16]
Therefore, the aim of this investigation is to do justice to both
detail and whole and thus gain the most objective view possible of
Shelley's application of imagery in his love poetry.

---

[16]Wasserman, Earl R.: *Shelley. A Critical Reading*. Baltimore - London 1971, p. vii.

CHAPTER I
IMAGES FOR THE BELOVED

The first part of "Epipsychidion" (lines 1-189) shows best
Shelley's search for an image apt to express the beauty and the
qualities of the adored beloved.   He tries to define her in terms
of image, shadow, reflection, and metaphor to give a hint at what
she might stand for, but only to come to the awareness:

> I measure
> The world of fancies, seeking one like thee,
> And find - alas! mine own infirmity.
>   Epips. 69-71

In fact, his inability to find a single adequate image arises from
his desire to define in human language what he considers divine -
an undertaking which naturally is doomed to failure.[17]   Therefore,
he has to turn to "a thousand images of loveliness", hoping that
they can express what one alone is unable to.[18]

---

[17]Cf. Wasserman, *Shelley* 428: "the poet represents what Shelley recurrently took to be the human dilemma, and the ecstatic in-
coherence of the metaphors for Emily and the inconsistency of what
she stands for arises, not from what she is, but from the irrecon-
cilable schism in man between his finite and infinite selves."

[18]Cf. Wilson, Milton: *Shelley's Later Poetry. A Study of His
Prophetic Imagination*. New York 1959, p. 223: "What Shelley seems
to have learned from this emphasis on the mortality of his poetic
medium is that since no figure is adequate, the poet's best chance
of defining his metaphysical target is to surround it with approxi-
mate ones.   He must converge on the target from a variety of angles."

1. "A SECOND SELF, FAR DEARER AND MORE FAIR"
   (Revolt, C.II.XXIV.875)
   (SHADOW - MIRROR - CIRCLE)

In the introductory Canto I of "The Revolt of Islam"[19], two
spirits return to the mighty Senate in the Temple of the Spirit
after the end of their mortal lives. From the first moment of
their appearance, Cythna, the female spirit and beloved of the narrative Cantos II till XII, is presented to the reader as her lover's
"shadow" (cf. C.I.LX.660). And indeed, Laon himself refers to her
as "mine own shadow" (C.II.XXIV.874), "a second self" (875; cf. "To
Harriet" (1812) 56). This idea reaches a climax when he later on
confesses: "She is my life, I am but the shade / Of her" (C.VIII.
XXV.3422-23). This is the ultimate possible expression of a lover
who denies the existence of his own genuine life if he looks at it
in relation to his beloved.

Likewise, the poet in "Epipsychidion" considers himself to be
part of Emily when he states: "I am not thine: I am a part of
thee" (Epips. 52).[20] The key to this at first look somewhat puz-

---

[19]C.I and XII are considered the frame, C.II till XI as the
explication - see Martinez, Alicia: *The Hero and Heroine of Shelley's
The Revolt of Islam* (= *Romantic Reassessment* 63) Salzburg 1976, p. 6;
for the symmetrical structure of the poem see Haswell, Richard H.:
"Shelley's The Revolt of Islam. The Connexion of its Parts": *KSJ*
25 (1976) 81-102; Martinez discovered yet another structural pattern
by examination of Shelley's 'historical perspective' - see *op. cit.*
p. 72ff.; - for a profound analysis of Canto I see Jones, Frederick
L.: "Canto I of The Revolt of Islam": *KSJ* 9 (1960) 27-33.

[20]The poet of "Epipsychidion" is a projection of Shelley himself - for a detailed treatment of this theme see Brown, Richard Edward: *Images of the Self in Shelley's Poetry*: DA 33 (1973) 5165A. -
see further Slater, John Frederick: *Edward Garnett: The 'Splendid
Advocate', 'Volpone' and 'Anthony and Cleopatra': The Play of Imagination, Self-Concealment and Self-Revelation in Shelley's 'Epipsychidion'*: DA 32 (1971) 3332A-3333A.

zling use of images to denote the relationship between lover and
beloved becomes clearer if we shift our attention to Shelley's essay "On Love", where he provides us with the clue to the comprehen-
sion of the underlying concept.

> We dimly see within our intellectual nature, a miniature
> as it were of our entire self, yet deprived of all that
> we condemn or despise, the ideal prototype of every-
> thing excellent and lovely that we are capable of con-
> ceiving as belonging to the nature of man. Not only
> the minutest principles of which our nature is com-
> posed; a mirror whose surface reflects not only the
> terms of purity and brightness, a soul within our soul
> that describes a circle around its proper paradise which
> pain and sorrow dare not overleap.[21]

In Cythna, in Emily, in fact in all women of his poems as well as
those with whom he fell in love in his private life, Shelley saw
the outward realization of man's self, the representation of his
prototype, yet purified from all negative qualities.

By applying the image of the shadow, Shelley causes some
dubiosity because he seems unable to make up his mind as to whether
the beloved is the lover's shadow or the other way round.[22]   From
another point of view also, this image does not seem to come up to
the meaning Shelley wanted to express.   If attributed to the
beloved, the shadow-image would denote that she is deprived of the
original splendour, is dim - as shadows usually are.   But this is
exactly the opposite of Shelley's intention.[23]   Therefore, this
image only works if it is used in the reverse way, namely by being
attributed to the male part of the relationship.   Then, conceiving
him as the shadow of some bright light would be a logical conclusion.

---

[21]Clark, *Prose* 170.

[22]Cf. the passages quoted above.

[23]Cf. Chapter I.2 - the beloved is associated with light and
splendour.

Another image already pointed out in the essay "On Love" is
that of the mirror, which is looked at under the aspect of its
reflective function. By reflecting purity and brightness the mirror itself appears pure and bright, indeed a manifestation of all
positive and ideal qualities. Thus, by "taking the mirror image
of himself and changing its sex, he also removes any flaws of wavy
lines of human limitation or imperfection. The result is not a
photographic reproduction but a highly idealistic work of art."[24]
Furthermore, Shelley calls the beloved a "soul within our soul", the
psyche's "epipsyche".[25] This concept is closely connected to the

------

[24]Leyda, Seraphia D.: *"Love's Rare Universe": Eros in Shelley's Poetry* (= *Explorations of Literature* 18) Baton Rouge 1966, 43-
69, p. 48; - for the development of Shelley's concept of the ideal
female, 'das Ideal-Weibliche', in his work see Maurer, Otto: *Shelley und die Frauen* (= *Literaturhistorische Forschungen* 33) Berlin-
Schöneberg 1906, p. 136; - for the concept of the 'Doppelgänger' see
Evans, James C.: "Masks of the Poet: A Study of Self-Confrontation
in Shelley's Poetry": *KSJ* 24 (1975) 70-89, especially p. 81 where
he considers the "Epipsychidion" to be the "full poetic treatment of
the Doppelgänger."

[25]For the meaning and the genesis of the word 'epipsyche' and
the title "Epipsychidion" see King-Hele, who explains it by referring
to Ptolemaic cosmology - "In the Ptolemaic cosmology the earth was
not fixed and the planets moved in epicycles or 'wheels upon wheels'.
Shelley builds up his title with the astronomical analogy in mind,
adds the Greek affectionate diminuitive -idion and replaces cycle by
psyche, so that Epi-psych-idion means 'a little soul upon a soul', a
Platonic inner soul. Finally, allowing for the oblique reference
to the Epithalamian convention we may translate 'Epipsychidion' as
'a song of praise about the little soul within the soul'". - King-
Hele, Desmond: *Shelley. His Thought and Work*. London 1964, p.
275; - cf. further Rogers, who renders Shelley's possible course of
thought as follows: "if you may have an Epinikon for a Triumph-song
and an Epithalamium for a Marriage-song, why should you not have an
Epipsychidion for a Soul-song? So, I think his mind worked and the
fact that ἐπιψύχη did not exist in Greek need not have troubled him
in his excited determination to write what would be an Epipsychidion."
-Rogers, *Shelley* 245; - Carey, too, considers the word 'epipsyche'
to have been formulated in analogy to 'epicycle' - see Carey, Gillian:

mirror and enriches the already established image by adding that of
circle and circumference. The "soul within the soul", the idealized
self, describes a circle around its proper paradise. Thus, both
images imply an active component: whilst the mirror-image is associated with reflection, the circle includes the element of radiance. By this radiant force an idealized and purified realm is
created, a paradise void of negative qualities like pain, sorrow,
and evil.

Let us now turn to the poems themselves to find affirmation
of the above.

Cythna is:

> *A second self, far dearer and more fair;*
> *Which clothed in undissolving radiancy*
> *All those steep paths which languour and despair*
> *Of human things, had made so dark and bare.*
>
> Revolt, C.II.XXIV.876-78

She is "far lovelier" (C.I.LX.661), a "purest being" (C.II.XXXII.
946), and therefore stands in sharp contrast to any kind of evil:

> *How without fear of evil or disguise*
> *Was Cythna! - what a spirit strong and mild,*
> *Which death, or pain, or peril would despise,*
> *Yet melt in tenderness! what genius wild*
> *Yet mighty, was enclosed within one simple child!*
>
> C.II.XXXII.950-54

In fact, the ideal female mind seems to have found "a sacred home"
in this woman of superlatives:

---

25 (cont'd) *Shelley* (= *Literature in Perspective*) London 1975,
p. 133; - for "this soul out of my soul" (Epips. 328) explained as
"a little additional soul" see Wasserman, *Shelley* 418; although the
theme of 'psyche-epipsyche' is most intensely developed in "Epipsychidion", it is personified in the figure of Panthea in Prometheus
Unbound; she is the image reflecting the past union of Prometheus
and Asia - see Marshall, William H.: "Plato's Myth of Aristophanes
and Shelley's Panthea": *Classical Journal* 55 (1960) 121-123.

Within that fairest form, the female mind
Untainted by the poison clouds which rest
On the dark world, a sacred home did find.
                              Revolt, C.II.XXXV.973-75

The "High, spirit-wingèd Heart" of "Epipsychidion" (13) - Emily -
is the perfect realization of the envisioned ideal woman (cf. Epips.
42: "Youth's vision thus made perfect"). And so, sure of the
positive response in advance, the poet can ask her,

              art thou not void of guile,
        A lovely soul formed to be blessed and bless?
                              Epips. 56-57

Here, the radiance of the ideal "soul within the soul" exists as a
blessing, the beloved embodies a circle of bliss into which the
lover enters by approaching her. Within this circumference he
participates in her purity in which his own better self is realized:

        In me, communion with this purest being
            Kindled intenser zeal, and made me wise
        In knowledge, which, in hers mine own mind seeing,
            Left in the world few mysteries:
                              C.II.XXXII.946-49

Thus, the lover's meeting with his 'epipsyche' is "the achievement
within himself of complete self-realization, of his best self. It
is the purging away of the accidental corruptions of earthly life
and enables the spark of the divine in him to stand forth in its
purity."[26]

        The poet in "Epipsychidion" becomes aware that he should have
entered this circumference of bliss much earlier,

        My spirit should at first have worshipped thine,
        A divine presence in a place divine.
                              Epips. 134-35

He knows about the purifying and renewing influence of his beloved's

-----

[26]Butter, *Idols* 43; cf. *ibid.* p. 12: "The mind knows itself,
realises its possibilities, only in action, in meeting. The only
thing in which it can see itself reflected is another mind...".

radiant spirit of beauty and good:

> *Thou Mirror*
> *In whom, as in the splendour of the Sun,*
> *All shapes look glorious which thou gazest on.*
>
> Epips. 30-32

At the same time he is conscious of the necessity of his own purity
if he wants to be worthy of her love and be an equal mate:

> *I love thee; yes, I feel*
> *That on the fountain of my heart a seal*
> *Is set, to keep its waters pure and bright*
> *For thee*
>
> Epips. 138-40

But a closer look at this relation of the lovers within this radiance soon shows that it is not one-sided, but a reciprocal one in
which both parts are passive as well as active and influence each
other to their mutual advantage.

Although Laon sees his own perfected self in Cythna, she, on
the other hand, is inspired by his ideas and strives for resemblance,

> *Whence came I what I am? thou, Laon, knowest*
> *How a young child should thus undaunted be;*
> *Methinks, it is a power which thou bestowest,*
> *Through which I seek, by most resembling thee,*
> *So to become most good, and great and free...*
>
> Revolt, C.II.XL.1018-22

In the "light of mutual love" (C.VIII.XXV.3421) man and woman
depend on each other:

> *In one another's substance finding food,*
> *Like flowers too pure and light and unimbued*
> *To nourish their bright lives with baser prey,*
> *Which point to Heaven and cannot pass away:*
>
> Epips. 580-83

It seems as if the radiance were no longer produced by one focus
only, describing a circle, but were of an elliptical shape with its
two focuses of male and female. Or, if taking up the other image,
it is a mirror reflecting the form in front of it.

Also in the short poem "To -, 'Yet look on me'", probably
dedicated to Mary, the recognition is a mutual one, lover and
beloved finding themselves in each other:

> *thou art alone,*
> *Like one before a mirror, without care*
> *Of aught but thine own features imaged there.*
>> 11. 7-9

Here, the mirror-image is combined with yet another one.   This is
the complementation of voice and its echo:

> *thy voice is as the tone*
> *Of my heart's echo*
>> 11. 5-6[27]

To sum up, we may say that "by seeing himself or herself perfected in the other and by trying to live up to the other's idea of
him or her, the lover may actually grow to be more like his or her
best possible self."[28]   In his private life, Shelley himself acted
according to this principle.   In a letter to Mary he once gave
voice to his delight about mutual influence and imitation.

> How divinely sweet a task it is, to imitate each
> other's excellences, and each moment to become wiser
> in this surpassing love - so that constituting but one
> being, all real knowledge may be comprised in the maxim
> γνωθι σεαυτον (know thyself) with infinitely more justice
> than its narrow and common application.[29]

The fact that one aspires to the qualities of the other is the
manifestation of their mutual fundamental experience of a void and
incompleteness, a deficiency implied in the sexual division of mankind.   Therefore, love, the unifying principle, is:

---

[27]Cf. Alastor, 153:   "Her voice was like the voice of his
own soul."

[28]Butter, *Idols* 11;   cf. Prom. Unb. IV.483-87:   "As a lover
or a chameleon / Grows like what it looks upon, / As a violet's
gentle eye / Gazes on the azure sky / Until its hue grows like what
it beholds."

[29]To Mary, Oct. 28, 1814;   *Letters* I.414.

> that powerful attraction towards all that we conceive,
> or fear, or hope beyond ourselves, when we find within
> our thoughts the chasm of an insufficient void and
> seek to awaken in all things that are a community with
> what we experience within ourselves.[30]

Love, therefore, desires not its opposite, but its complement; and
the lovers - though different - are meant to form a harmonious
entity:

> We - are we not formed as notes of music are,
> For one another, though dissimilar;
> Such difference without discord...
>
> Epips. 142-44

Whereas Laon embodies reason and intellect, Cythna is the embodiment of passion and love.   Different from the conventional role
division of sexes, Laon is associated with passivity and Cythna
represents the active force.   Thus, in their common task of reform-
ing the world, their characters stand for the two modes in which it
can be achieved - passive resistance and active force.   Both Laon
and Cythna are dependent on each other.   Cythna is the source of
inspiration for Laon's political ideas and his poetic work.   He
then conveys his conceptions to his beloved counterpart, who becomes the active disseminator of his thoughts.   This way, their
"supporting and enriching insights ... make up a new creative synthesis"[31], and their final union marks the reconciliation of activity and passivity, wisdom and passion, sympathy and love.

------

[30]"On Love"; Clark, *Prose* 170; cf. the influence on Shelley
of Diotima's lesson to Socrates in Plato's "Symposium": "Love,
therefore, and everything else that desires anything, desires that
which is absent and beyond its reach, that which it has not, that
which is not itself, that which it wants; such are the things of
which there are desire and love." - quoted from Martinez, *Hero and
Heroine* 43; - Eros in Shelley's poetry is consistently characterized
by sympathy and the 'void' - see Leyda, *Romantic Love* 15.

[31]McNiece, Gerald: *Shelley and the Revolutionary Idea.*
Cambridge - Massachusetts 1969, p. 199.

This experience of a void is most vehemently felt by a poet-hero who is "possessed / With thoughts too swift and strong for one lone human breast" (Revolt, C.IX.XXXIII.3764-65). Consequently, the lack of communion leads to solitude, "a sense of loneliness, a thirst with which I pined" (Revolt, Ded., V.45), and

> This misery was but coldly felt, till she
> Became my only friend, who had endowed
> My purpose with a wider sympathy.
> Revolt, C.II.XXXVI.982-84[32]

He is, then,

> no more alone through the world's wilderness,
> no more companionless,
> Where solitude is like despair
> Revolt, Ded., VIII.64.66-67

The finding of his ideal prototype is therefore, first of all, a communion and commingling of thoughts, which strips the desperate mood from the poet's lonely heart:

> And this beloved child thus felt the sway
> Of my conceptions, gathering like a cloud
> The very wind on which it rolls away;
> Hers too were all my thoughts, ere yet endowed
> With music and with light, their fountains flowed
> In poesy...
> Revolt, C.II.XXXI.937-42

As already indicated, Shelley believed that "the self ... cannot be

---

[32] Cf. Leyda, *Eros* 43: "Sympathy has two faces in Shelley's poetry. With one face it looks upon all things and creatures in the universe and uncritically embraces them. With its other face, sympathy views all things and finds them alien. It focuses upon human kind and seldom sees a man or woman who can respond to the feeling or return the understanding which it so urgently presses upon them. This situation leads to the experience of the 'void' and, consequently, to the motif of solitude and possible destruction." - Shelley himself could not endure solitude - cf. his letter to Hogg, May 8, 1811; *Letters* I.77: "I cannot endure the horror, the evil which comes to self in solitude."

content with exploring its own dens"[33], and love, therefore, is "a
going out of our own nature and an identification with the beautiful
which exists in thought, action, or person, not our own."[34] The
enemy of love, consequently, is self-love[35], and because Laon and
the poet in "Epipsychidion" do not seek their counterpart in "self-
centered seclusion" the 'psyche - epipsyche' relationship in these
two poems "can be viewed as a comment on the failure of the Poet in
Alastor."[36]

Although the search for the ideal 'epipsyche' is characterized
by the quest for those qualities which the 'psyche' itself does not
possess, it is also marked by the desire to find its likeness.   In
his essay "On Love", Shelley described this feature when he remarked:

> We are born into the world, and there is something
> within us which, from the instant we live, more and
> more thirsts after its likeness.[37]

This resemblance is to comprise all three aspects of human life:
reason, imagination, and emotion:

> If we reason, we would be understood; if we imagine,
> we would that the airy children of our brain be born
> anew within another's; if we feel, we would that
> another's nerves should vibrate to our own, that the
> beams of their eyes should kindle at once and mix and
> melt into our own, that lips of motionless ice should
> not reply to lips quivering and burning with the heart's

---

[33]Wilson, *Later Poetry* 149.

[34]"Defence of Poetry"; Clark, *Prose* 282f.

[35]Cf. Wilson, *Later Poetry* 155: "Love (and its herold imagination) is centrifugal; self-love is centripedal.   Love strives to
push back, or expand beyond, the circumference.   Self-love grows
inward and presses upon the center."; for 'self' and compounds in
Shelley's poetry cf. Ellis, *Concordance* 579f.

[36]Ruff, James Lynn: *Shelley's The Revolt of Islam* (= *Romantic
Reassessment* 10) Salzburg 1972, p. 57.

[37]Clark, *Prose* 170.

blood.   That is Love.[38]

This corresponds exactly to what Shelley called "not only the por-
trait of our external being, but an assemblage of the minutest
principles of which our nature is composed."[39]

>This search for the likeness is necessary because,
>
>Neither the eye nor the mind can see itself unless
>reflected upon that which it resembles.[40]

And this resemblance is most likely to exist if the lovers have the
same mother, if they are brother and sister.   This is the true
reason for Shelley's application of the incest-motif, which was a
popular one in Shelley's days and but one aspect of romantic love.[41]

---

[38]"On Love";   Clark, *Prose* 170;   for the influence of Plato's
'Ladder of Love' in the 'Symposium' see Stempel, Daniel: "Shelley
and the Ladder of Love":   *KSJ* 15 (1966) 15-23 - the ladder comprises
three stages: intellectual love, the understanding which unites two
minds with similar ideas;   love as imagination on the level of arts
and of its source, imagination (this is symbolized by the change
from words to song and music as the medium of communication) and
sensation, physical desire, and consumation (cf. p. 16);   for Plato's
influence on Shelley in general cf. the excellent study of Woodman,
Ross G.:   "Shelley's Changing Attitude to Plato":   *Journal of the
History of Ideas* 31 (1960) 497-510.

[39]"On Love";   Clark, *Prose* 170.

[40]"Defence of Poetry";   Clark, *Prose* 285.

[41]Cf. Maurer, *Frauen* 70f.;   cf. Martinez, *Hero and Heroine* 60:
"In terms of the concept of the epipsyche, an incestuous union would
be the most perfect.";   similar Leyda, *Romantic Love* 261:   "Incest
becomes a factor in increasing the possibility of likeness and, consequently, the chances of a successful relationship.   The 'sister'
motif in Shelley's concept of eros is one aspect of the epipsychidion,
the 'soul of my soul'.";   possible sources for Shelley's concept of
incest may have been: Wieland, *Agathon;*   Lawrence, *Empire of the
Nairs;*   Byron, *Abydos;*   Godwin, *Mandeville;*   Lewis, *Monk;*   Hunt,
Story of Rimini - see King-Hele, *Thought* 136;   see further Rogers,
Shelley 231:   in Wieland's *Agathon* the brother-sister relationship
exists between Agathon (the Platonic philosopher) and Psyche (the
ideal embodiment of Beauty).

Originally, Laon and Cythna were brother and sister, and although Shelley had to change this motif after the first publication of the poem and insert 'lover' and 'friend' instead of 'brother' and 'sister', the thematical substance remained unaltered.[42]

> *- the youthful years*
> *Which we together passed, their hopes and fears,*
> *The blood itself[43] which ran within our frames,*
> *That likeness of the features which endears*
> *The thoughts expressed by them ...*
>
> Revolt, C.VI.XXXI.2608-12

Therefore, their union of two resembling personalities is a successful one, standing out among many others:

> *Few were the living hearts, which could unite*
> *Like ours, or celebrate a bridal night*
> *With such close sympathies, for they had sprung*
> *From linked youth, and from the gentle might*
> *Of earliest love, delayed and cherished long,*
> *Which common hopes and fears made, like a tempest, strong.*
>
> C.VI.XXXIX.2680-85

Likewise, in "Epipsychidion" the poet addresses Emily as "Sweet Spirit! Sister of that orphan one" (1).[44] And even more he desires that they would have been twins, the closest relationship possible:

> *Would we two have been twins of the same mother!*
>
> Epips. 45

---

[42] For the changing of the original text of "Laon and Cythna" see Shelley's letter to Thomas Moore, Dec. 16, 1817; *Letters* I.435 and Blunden, Edmund: *Shelley. A Life Story.* London 1948, p. 166; cf. Ruff, *Revolt* 60: "Their relationship obviously duplicates that of the Woman and Serpent of canto I, who fused together into an androgynous figure."; for the meaning of the names 'Laon' and 'Cythna' cf. *ibid.* p. 60ff.; on Cythna's second name 'Laone' Ruff comments thus: "Though not grammatical Greek, Laone is obviously Shelley's attempt to identify Cythna with Laon. As Laon's epipsyche, she also represents the ideals and hopes of the people." - *ibid.* p. 62.

[43] Originally, "The common blood" - see Freydorf, *Bildhafte Sprache* 56/40.

[44] Adolfo de Bosis, Shelley's Italian translator, pointed out that the 'orphan one' is not Mary, but the spirit of Shelley - see Rogers, *Shelley* 236.

And in expectation of the forthcoming union he can proclaim:

> *We shall become the same, we shall be one*
> *Spirit within two frames, oh! wherefore two?*
> *One passion in twin-hearts...*
>
> Epips. 573-75[45]

The poet's relation to Emily appears quite obscure for he seems
to see in her his sister as well as his bride when he calls her
"Spouse! Sister!" (130) at the same time. This double considera-
tion also marks his invitation to sail with him to their chosen isle:

> *The day is come, and thou wilt fly with me.*
> *To whatso'er of dull mortality*
> *Is mine, remain a vestal sister still;*
> . . . .
> *   henceforth be thou united*
> *Even as a bride, delighting and delighted.*
>
> Epips. 388-93[46]

Whether one or the other term is to be understood symbolically, cannot be decided, and Shelley himself leaves the question open when he
comments on this passage in a fragment to the poem:

> *If any should be curious to discover*
> *Whether to you I am a friend or lover,*
> *Let them read Shakespeare's sonnets[47], taking thence*
> *A whetstone for their dull intelligence*
> *That tears and will not cut them, or let them guess*
> *How Diotima, the wise prophetess,*

---

[45]Cf. Fiordispina, 11-16:
"They were two cousins, almost like two twins,
Except that from the catalogue of sins
Nature had rased their love- which could not be
But by dissevering their nativity
And so they grew together like two flowers
Upon one stem."

[46]Cf. further Epips. 491-92: "a pleasure-house / Made sacred
to his sister and his spouse".

[47]Cf. Rogers, *Shelley* 232: "Shelley's use of the word 'friend'
both in poems and in correspondence addressed to women is exactly in
correspondence with the spiritualized conception of the word which he
understood to be present in Shakespeare's sonnets."

Instructed the instructor, and why he
Rebuked the infant spirit of melody
On Agathon's sweet lips, which as he spoke
Was as the lovely star when morn has broke
The roof of darkness, in the golden dawn,
Half-hidden, and yet beautiful.
                              I'll pawn
My hopes of Heaven - you know what they are worth -
That the presumptuous pedagogues of Earth,
If they could tell the riddle offered here
Would scorn to be, or being to appear
What now they seem and are - but let them chide,
They have few pleasures in the world beside;
Perhaps we should be dull were we not chidden,
Paradise fruits are sweetest when forbidden.
Folly can season Wisdom, Hatred Love.
                                    Fr. Epips. 79-117[48]

The search for the ideal prototype who is the manifestation - as we

have found out - of likeness and complementation is a fundamental

element of Shelley's concept of 'psyche' and 'epipsyche'.   It is

---

[48]On the leaf before the manuscript of the Dedication to "The
Revolt of Islam", Shelley had copied in his notebook Salomon's Song
of Songs Cap. 4-v.9 - cf. particularly 4.v.12 or Cap. 5.v.2: "Thou
hast revisited my heart, my sister, my spouse..."; "A garden en-
closed is my sister, my spouse..."; "... it is the voice of my
beloved that knocketh, saying, open to me my sister, my love, my
dove, my undefiled." - see Wasserman, *Shelley* 420; as a parallel to
Epips. 45 ("Would we two have been twins of the same mother") cf.
the wish of Salomon's bride, Song of Songs 8,1: "O that thou wert
as my brother, that sucked the breasts of my mother! When should I
find thee without, I would kiss thee; yea, I should not be despised."
- see *ibid.* p. 421; the address 'sister' and 'brother' is also to be
found in nature - e.g. Prom. Unb. IV.325 (moon to earth: "brother
mine"), IV.467 ("brother"), Asia, Panthea, and Ione are sisters; cf.
also Love's Philosophy, II.9-14:
          "See the mountains kiss high Heaven
          And the waves clasp one another;
          No sister flower could be forgiven
          If it disdained its brother.
          And the sunlight clasps the earth
          And the moonbeams kiss the sea."

most tellingly illustrated in the second part of "Epipsychidion" (lines 190-320), in which the poet realizes this "going out of our- selves", and enters "Into the wintry forest of our life" (249; cf. "world's wilderness" in Revolt, Ded., VIII.64) to find the incarna- tion of the "Being whom my spirit oft / Met on its visioned wander- ings" (Epips. 190-91).[49]

He sets forth and questions

> *every tongueless wind that flew*
> . . . .
> *Whither 'twas fled, this soul out of my soul;*
> Epips. 236.38[50]

In many mortal forms he tries to find his 'epipsyche':

> *In many mortal forms I rashly sought*
> *The shadow of that idol of my thought.*
> Epips. 267-68[51]

---

[49]Cf. Butter, *Idols* 40: "it (i.e. "Epips.") is the story of the lover's, any lover's search for an eventual finding of his per- fect soul-mate."

[50]The First Canzone from Dante's Convito is closely related to "Epipsychidion"; its central thought appears in the fourth stanza and it is that of the soul of the lover going out to meet the beloved - Shelley translated it thus:
"Thou art not dead, but thou hast wandered,
Thou Soul of ours, who thyself dost fret"
see Rogers, *Shelley* 233; for a parallel between "Epipsychidion" and the Song of Songs see Wasserman, *Shelley* 422f.: Song of Songs 3,1: "By night on my bed I sought him whom my soul loveth, I sought him, but I found him not."; 3, 2-4: "I will rise now and in the broad ways I will seek him whom my soul loveth: I sought him, but I found him not. The watchmen that go about the city found me: to whom I said, Saw ye him whom my soul loveth? It was but a little that I passed from them, but I found him whom my soul loveth: I told him, and would not let him go, until I had brought him into my mother's house, and into the chamber of her that conceived me."

[51]This is a "direct allusion to the parable of the cave in Plato's *Republic*, where imprisoned mortals see only shadows cast on the inner walls by idols moving past the entrance" - King-Hele, *Thought* 275; Rogers supposes Shelley to have adopted a phrase of Aeschylus - see Rogers, *Shelley* 63/1: "πολλῶν ὀνομάτων - μορφὴ μία" - "One form, under many names".

The lover strives through the universe, which has become a chaos (cf. Epips. 234), and his path is beset with error and delusion:

> And struggling through its error with vain and strife,
> And stumbling in my weakness and my haste,
> And half-bewildered by new forms, I passed
> Seeking among those untaught foresters
> If I could find one form resembling hers,
> In which she might have masked herself from me.
>
> Epips. 250-55

This diversity of forms stands in sharp contrast to the one which the poet desires to find.   Thus here - as elsewhere in Shelley's poetry - the variegated forms are one image in which evil masks itself.

The symbolic landscapes through which the poet passes indicate various states of mind he has to go through.   First, he meets "One, whose voice was venomed melody" (Epips. 256), sitting "by a well, under blue nightshade bowers" (257).   She is the incarnation of isolated (and therefore destructive) sensual lust.[52]   Her breath is "like faint flowers" (258) and,

> from her living cheeks and bosom flew
> A killing air which pierced like honey-dew
> Into the core of my green heart, and lay
> Upon its leaves ...
>
> Epips. 261-64

The images used here are a parody of those in the first part when Emily is described (compare 1. 83 to 1. 270 and 1. 109 to 11. 262-66).

The outward similarity is dangerous for the poet because it is apt to mislead him into even greater misery instead of offering deliverance:

---

[52]So Butter, *Idols* 16 and Leyda, *Eros* 63:   "Sensual love alone is deadly;   it poisons the well of being rather than feeds and sustains it."

> *Then as a hunted deer that could not flee,*
> *I turned upon my thoughts, and stood at bay,*
> *Wounded and weak and panting; the cold day*
> *Trembled, for pity of my strife and pain.*
> Epips. 272-75

Next, he comes across astronomical images which promise to bring
this deliverance, but do not prove true either.[53]   The "cold
chaste Moon", "whose changes ever run / Into themselves"[54] is a
"shrine of soft yet icy flame", which "warms but not illumines"
(cf. Epips. 279-85).   This impression of cold is further emphasized
by her "silver voice" (301).

This state is also spoken of in "To Constantia", dedicated to
Claire Claremont:

> *The rose that drinks the fountain dew*
> *In the pleasant air of noon,*
> *Grows pale and blue with altered hue -*
> *In the gaze of the nightly moon;*
> *For the planet of frost, so cold and bright,*
> *Makes it wan with her borrowed light.*
> I. 1-6

Also the "Comet beautiful and fierce" (Epips. 368) cannot fulfill
the poet's desire - this task is reserved for the "living Sun" with

---

[53]Cf. Wasserman, *Shelley* 234: "the astronomical imagery
recapitulated from the first movement enters as secondary metaphors
into a context in which the primary metaphor is the forest of life
but rapidly displaces the forest metaphor to constitute a total universe of earth, sun, moon, and star.   The imagery which the poet,
in his ecstasy, had huddled chaotically together and tried to unite
in Emily is being sorted out and distributed into a cosmos."   For
the images used for Emily in the first part of "Epipsychidion" see
Chapter I.2.

[54]For the significance of this and other reflexive images in
this passage see Keach, William: "Reflexive Imagery in Shelley":
KSJ 24 (1975) 49-69, p. 59f.; see further Wasserman, *Shelley* 434:
"is the spirit of eternally repetitive cyclical change, the principle of temporal perfection in the realm of mutability."

its "urn of golden fire" (375-76).[55]   Thus, the quest which started
in the "wintry forest of life", went through tempests and earth-
quakes, finally enters into "the dawn of the long night" (341),
where it finds its haven amidst "flowers as soft as thoughts of
budding love" (328), and the poet hears "the small, still spirit of
that sound" (331).[56]

----

[55]Butter considers Sun, Moon, and Comet to be states of mind
rather than people but does not exclude the validity of both ex-
planations; he further comments that, "The sun symbolizes the goal
towards which he has been striving; but Moon and Comet ... are not
evil.   The Moon, though cold, reflects the light of the Sun, and
the Comet, though it can be destructive, also contains light.   In
the final state, the different parts of the soul - Imagination,
Reason, Emotion - are to exist together in harmony." - Butter, *Idols*
18; Carey associates the planets with persons only - "it is clear
that Mary is represented by the Moon and Emilia by the Sun; but the
identification of the 'One whose voice was venomed melody' (I.256)
or the Comet (I.368) is perplexing." - Carey, *Shelley* 133; cf.
Rogers, *Shelley* 232: Emily is "the culmination of the series of
women pursued in his quest, is hung with the trophies of her prede-
cessors: he refers to them cryptically in the poem but it does not
really matter, for instance, what woman of the past was the 'Comet
beautiful and fierce' nor who had the voice which was 'venomed
melody': Emilia now comprehends them all.   She is the symbol of
love itself."; similar King-Hele, *Thought* 276: "This string of
obscure figures is usually treated as a list of Shelley's lady-
loves.   The 'true' one is then Harriet Grove, the Moon is Mary, the
Sun is Emilia and the Comet Clare.   The lady of electric poison and
the Tempest-Planet remain unidentified." - For a detailed study of
the Planet-Tempest passage see Cameron, Kenneth Neill: "The Planet-
Tempest Passage in Epipsychidion": *PMLA* 63 (1948) 950-972.

[56]Wasserman found out the existing parallel between this passage and I Kings 19 - "The pattern of the narrative that has begun
with the cataclysmic tempest and earthquake and ends with the 'small,
still, sweet spirit' of Emily's respiration is borrowed from I Kings
19." - Wasserman, *Shelley* 437; there, the prophet Elijah (like the
poet of "Epips.") entered a cave - "And behold, the Lord passed by,
and a great strong wind rent the mountain, and brake in pieces the
rocks before the Lord; but the Lord was not in the wind: and after
the wind an earthquake; but the Lord was not in the earthquake:

In a similar way, the description of scenery in "The Revolt of Islam" corresponds to and signifies happenings in the minds. Before Laon and Cythna can be united and thus celebrate the successful search for the 'epipsyche', they have to undergo redemption and purification - Laon in a tower overlooking the sea, and Cythna in a cave with a fountain (cf. Cantos III and VII). Both symbols and their surrounding scenery are images for the lovers' mental states.[57]

---

[56] (cont'd) And after the earthquake, a fire; but the Lord was not in the fire; and after the fire a still small voice." (quoted *ibid*. p. 437); cf. Epips. 336-38 (vision of Emily): "This glorious One / Floated into the cavern where I lay, / And called my Spirit" - cf. on hearing God's still voice Elijah "went out, and stood in the entering of the cave. And, behold, there came a voice unto him, and said, What doest thou here, Elijah?" (quoted *ibid*. p. 347); for the significance of 'cave' cf. Freydorf, Bildhafte Sprache 110: "Ruhe bedeutet für Shelley, den Motoriker, nur 'sich bewegt haben' und 'zu neuer Bewegung auf dem Sprunge sein'. Zu solcher Ruhe legen sich alle Gestalten seiner Schöpfung in einer Höhle nieder...".

[57] "In both cases, Shelley uses images of imprisonment to symbolize states of the mind or spirit; Laon is chained on a tower, and Cythna is locked in a cave." - Ruff, *Revolt* 69f.; Ruff considers Cythna's cave to be the cave of her mind - cf. *ibid*. p. 76, and the fountain in it to be a source of life (p. 78); cf. further Butter, *Idols* 46: "The mind may be a wilderness with many paths or a cave with many chambers, or, more commonly, it may be a whole landscape with cave, whirlpools, woods, etc."; for the two symbolic uses of 'cave' see *ibid*. p. 60; fountains suggest inspiration, wisdom, or something of the kind springing up within the mind (*ibid*. p. 56).

2. "FAIR STAR OF LOVE AND LIFE"[58]
(Revolt, C.IX.XXXVI.3788)

(STAR - LAMP - SHADOW - VEIL)

The series of "rhapsodically chaotic"[59] imagery in the first
movement of "Epipsychidion" (lines 1-189) seems to be "inexhaustible
to analysis"[60], not least for its beauty and splendour. Although
somewhat confusing because of their being intermixed, all the
images used to address Emily share a common underlying principle.
They are uttered in a state of praise and awe in the glow of the
beloved's brightness, her countenance of light. Emily is associated with and described in terms of light - no matter whether
natural or artificial, because the effect remains the same.

She is figured as the "Seraph of Heaven" (Epips. 21), a
"veiled Glory" (26), and a "Star" (28.60). She is compared to the
"splendour of the Sun" (31), she is an "Incarnation of the Sun"
(335), and she is herself called "a Splendour" (116).[61] Another

---

[58]Cf. Rogers, *Shelley* 107: This is "a translation of an epigram of Plato's where the lover is conceiving his love as a micro-
cosm of the all-pervading spirit of World Love"; the epigram runs
thus: Ἀστέρας εἰσαθρεῖς Ἀστὴρ ἐμός. εἴθε γενοίμην οὐρανός, ὡς
πολλοῖς ὄμμασιν εἰς σὲ βλέπω.

[59]Wasserman, *Shelley* 426; cf. Leyda, *Eros* 55: "a compendium
of ecstatic images in praise of Emily".

[60]Bloom, Harold: *Shelley's Mythmaking*. New York 1969, p. 214.

[61]By picturing Emily as a celestial light, Shelley makes use
of his "persistent symbol of the immortal soul and of those perfec-
tions he associates with it, love and life." - Wasserman, *Shelley*
424; cf. Salama, Adel: *Shelley's Major Poems. A Re-Interpretation*
(= *Romantic Reassessment* 9) Salzburg 1973, p. 213: "Surely the fusion of Platonic and Dantesque elements in the metaphysical back-
ground of this passage is unmistakable."; 'Seraph of Heaven' is
"Shelley's variant of Beatrice".

time the poet addresses her as "Sweet Lamp!" (153).   It seems as
if he tried to find all synonyms for 'light' to express the impression which Emily's presence left on him.

In the "Revolt of Islam" the effect of Cythna on Laon must
have been similar.   She is presented as "a shape of brightness"
(C.II.XXIII.865), "a child of glory" (C.II.XXVIII.918; cf. XXXVII.
991), whose "wondrous loveliness" (C.VII.V.2866) causes Laon to address her in a sway of ecstasy as the "Fair star of love and life"
(C.IX.XXXVI.3788; cf. Ded., I.9: "thou child of love and light").

All this glory of the beloved - produced by her external as
well as internal, spiritual beauty - has the same expanding, dif-
fusing, and penetrating power, as it is the characteristic feature
of light.   And like light effluencing from its source (lamp, star,
etc.) the woman - though herself the embodiment of brightness -
also has a circle of splendour around her countenance; she radiates
light and thus causes influence on the world surrounding her.[62]

> She moved upon this earth a shape of brightness
>   A power, that from its objects scarcely drew
> One impulse of her being - in her brightness
>   Most like some radiant cloud of morning dew
>   Which wanders through the waste air's pathless blue,
> To nourish some far desert.
>   Revolt, C.II.XXIII.865-70

Thus, "Cythna's pure and radiant self" (C.III.III.1132) is "like a
spirit through the darkness shining" (C.V.LII.2274).   Wherever she

---

[62]Cf. Salama, *Major Poems* 216: "This form of woman is a
centre from which the divine light is diffused in extending circles
which ultimately enclose the world."; Wasserman, *Shelley* 425:
"this 'intense Diffusion', blurring the outlines of her finiteness,
flows round her, even to her finger tips, which in turn quiver with
the throbbing blood as the light in the morning pulsates through
snowy clouds."; for the influence of the scientist Adam Walker,
who identified electricity, light, and heat, on Shelley's inter-
changeable use of these images, see Butter, *Idols* 145.

appears, she penetrates "like the phantom of the dawn, / A spirit from the caves of daylight" (C.XII.VIII.420-21) the dark night of the world and fills it with a brighter atmosphere, a spark from some eternal sun.

> *that Beauty ...*
> *Which penetrates and clasps and fills the world*
> Epips. 102-3

> *- and a light*
> *Of liquid tenderness, like love, did rise*
> *From her whole frame, an atmosphere which quite*
> *Arrayed her in its beams, tremulous and soft and bright.*
> Revolt, C.XI.V.4266-69

"Clothed in the radiance undefiled" (Revolt, Ded., XII.104), Cythna is "like an Angel robed in white" (C.VI.XIX.2502);[63] and Emily, too, is "robed in such exceeding glory" (Epips. 199).[64]

Clothed in such bright garments, she contrasts with this dim earthly realm. She is not only the "Sweet Benediction in the eternal Curse", but even more the "Veiled Glory of this lampless Universe", the "Moon beyond the clouds", a "living Form among the Dead", a "Star above the storm" (cf. Epips. 25-29). Furthermore, she is,

> *a Star*
> *Which moves not in the moving heavens alone*[65]

---

[63]Cf. "her star-bright robe" in C.I.XVIII.295.

[64]Cf. Fragment: Beauty's Halo, 1-2: "Thy beauty hangs around thee like / Splendour around the moon."

[65]Cf. Kroese, Irvin B.: *The Beauty and the Terror: Shelley's Visionary Women* (= *Romantic Reassessment* 23) Salzburg 1976, p. 94f.: "This distinction hinges on Emily as the image of a static, unchanging reality and that of an active, pervading effluence"; like Ebbinghaus, Wilhelm: *Das Aesthetische Einheits- und Vollkommenheitsproblem bei Shelley.* Marburg 1931, p. 11: "inmitten der Mannigfaltigkeit und Veränderlichkeit, die sich ihrerseits notwendig in Bewegung vollzieht, ist die Freundin als Stern das Eine und In-sich-Ruhende. Sie ist gleichsam 'ruhender Pol' inmitten einer

> *A Smile amid dark frowns, a gentle voice*
> *Amid rude voices, a beloved light.*
> Epips. 60-63[66]

But however great the contrast may be, this "Radiant Sister of the
Day" (Jane, Invit. 47) cannot be content with only being the source
of and dweller within her light. Her aim must be to overcome the
existing contrast by changing the opposite into her own glorious
being:

> *Thou Mirror*
> *In whom, as in the splendour of the Sun,*
> *All shapes look glorious which thou gazest on.*
> Epips. 30-32[67]

> *The glory of her being, issuing thence*
> *Stains the dead, blank, cold air with a warm shade*

-----

[65] (cont'd)mannigfaltigen und bewegten Welt, eines, 'chaos
in commotion' (Fragm. 65)"; see further Revolt, Ded., XIV.121-24,
where Shelley and Mary are compared to "two tranquil stars, while
clouds are passing by"; see also Adonais, LII. 460-61: "The One
remains, the many change and pass; / Heaven's light forever shines,
Earth's shadows fly".

[66]Wasserman pointed out the parallel between these opposites
and a passage from the Song of Songs - "The model for Shelley's
opening series of metaphors for Emily is Salomon's 'As the lily
among thorns, so is my love among the daughters' and the bride's
reply, 'As the apple among the trees of the world, so is my beloved
among the sons' (2:2-3). Frequently interpreted to mean spiritual
perfection in the midst of worldly wickedness, these similes provide
a metaphoric pattern on which Shelley could play variations to
represent the embodiment of spiritual perfection in the mortal condition." - Wasserman, *Shelley* 422; see further Leyda, *Eros* 58:
"The contrast between the world as it exists and the world created
by love serves as foundation for most of the complimentary images
addressed to Emily."

[67]Cf. Dante's *La Vita Nuova*, XXI: "In her eyes my lady
beareth Love. Wherefore what she looketh upon is gentle made.";
also Canzoniere III: "Her beauty reins down flameless of fire made
living by a gentle spirit which is the creator of every good thought;
and they scatter like thunder the inborn vices that make folk vile."
- quoted from: Salama, *Major Poems* 213.

*Of unentangled intermixture, made
By Love, of light and motion.*
                    Epips. 91-94[68]

She leaves the same effect on the world in general as she leaves
upon her lover:

*in her beauty's glow
I stood, and felt the dawn of my long night
Was penetrating me with living light.*
                    Epips. 340-42

Within this radiant and transfigural activity, the beloved's eyes
function predominantly.   Though her whole body is radiating light,
her eyes seem to be the epicenter, the inmost core of the glory issued forth.

Cythna's "dark and deepening eyes, / Which, as twin phantoms
of one star lies / O'er a dim well" (Revolt, C.VI.XXXIII. 2626-28)
are "too earnest and too sweet ever to be denied" (C.II.XXVI.899-
900), because they are the fountain and the planet from which the
waters and beams of the light of love spring.

*from the eyes whose deepest light
Of love and sadness made my lips feel pale
    With influence strange of mournfullest delight,
My own sweet Cythna looked*
                    Revolt, C.VI.XXIV.2546-49

*she bent
Her looks on mine; those eyes a kindling beam
Of love divine into my spirit sent*
                    C.I.XXIV.339-41

The secret seems to lie in "a lamp of vestal fire burning internal-
ly" (Revolt, Ded., XI.99), which makes its way through the beloved's
eyes to meet and penetrate the lover beholding the woman's beauty.
This effect and influence of someone's - especially a beloved woman's

---
[68]Fraser considers this to be "a wonderful passage fusing an
intellectual excitement, an idealistic vision, ... with an intense
sensuous eroticism." - Fraser, G. S.: *P. B. Shelley. Adonais, Epipsychidion: Notes on Literature* 79 (1968) p. 9.

- eyes is one of Shelley's characteristic images and can be traced throughout his poetry. Thus, it is a common motif even in his shorter poems.[69]

In "To Constantia, Singing", dedicated to Claire Claremont, he asks his beloved,

> *Constantia, turn!*
> *In thy dark eyes a power like light doth lie.*
> I.2-3

Likewise, Harriet's eyes are "Beaming with mildest radiance on my heart" ("To Harriet", 1812, 53), because a "warm sunshine" ("To Harriet", 1814, 8) is being issued forth from them.

Feeling his beloved's look upon him, the lover experiences a transfiguration of the world in which earth and heaven are fused:

> *Wilt thou not turn*
> *Those spirit-beaming eyes and look on me*
> *Until I be assured that Earth is Heaven,*
> *And Heaven is Earth?*
> To Harriet (1812) 11-13

This being raised above the present empirical state is possible because of the healing and calming influence of the woman's eyes.

> *Thy look of love has power to calm*
> *The stormiest passion of my soul.*
> To Harriet (1814) 1-2

> *thy dark eyes threw*
> *Their soft persuasion on my brain,*
> *Charming away its dream of pain.*
> To Mary Wollstonecraft Godwin,
> IV.22-24

Associated with the radiating force of the eyes is their magnetic power: Cythna's eyes,

---

[69]Cf. Leyda, *Romantic Love* 169: "The 'eyes' in Shelley's love poetry and the lights, the arrows, the lightnings which flash from them are images for the communication of that love and sympathy which words are incapable of expressing."

> *Were lodestars of delight, which drew me home*
> *When I might wander forth.*
>> Revolt, C.II.XXI.847-48

By attracting the lover they function in the same way as a lamp
upon a moth.   The poet in "Epipsychidion" flitted

> *towards the lodestar of my own desire*
> *..... like a dizzy moth, whose flight*
> *Is as a dead leaf's in the owlet light*
>> Epips. 219-21[70]

and in identifying Emily with the lamp he can exclaim,

> *Sweet Lamp! my moth-like muse has burnt its wings.*
>> Epips. 53 [71]

The beloved's smile functions similarly; it, too, is the source of
light, and it has the power of transfiguration.

> *delight*
> *And exultation, and a joyance free,*
> *Solemn, serene, and lofty, filled the light*
> *Of the calm smile with which she looked on me.*
>> Revolt, C.III.VIII.1171-75

> *A sweet and solemn smile, like Cythna's, cast*
> *One moment's light, which made my heart beat fast.*
>> C.V.XXIV.1930-31

> *She turned to me and smiled - that smile was Paradise!*
>> C.IX.XXXVI.3792

As the beholding of the beloved's eyes can make heaven and earth
meet, so her smile can create a paradise; it can, in fact, fore-
shadow and manifest heaven's beauty in mortal life.

Endowed with all these splendid qualities, she transcends

------

[70]Cf. "To -, 'One word is too often profaned'", II.9-10.13:
"I can give not what men call love. / But wilt thou accept not /
The desire of the moth for the star."

[71]Freydorf comments on this image, "In dem Augenblick ..., in
dem das Tier symbolisch für einen Menschen steht, gewinnt es etwas
wie Eigenleben. Der dem Licht zufliegende Nachtfalter wird, wie
andere beflügelte Tiere, häufig zum Sinnbild für einen Menschen."
- Freydorf, *Bildhafte Sprache* 113.

herself and shows the way to something or someone beyond.

> As one who feels an unseen spirit
> Is my heart when thine is near it.
>
> To Sophia (Miss Stacey) IV.23-24

The lover experiences,

> The shadow which doth float unseen,
> But not unfelt, o'er blind mortality.
>
> Revolt, C.VI.XXXVII.2659-60

He beholds the beloved as:

> a mortal shape indued
> With love and light and deity,
> And motion which may change but cannot die.
>
> Epips. 112-14

And going one step further, he doubts that she should be human only when he exclaims,

> Seraph of Heaven! too gentle to be human,
> Veiling beneath that radiant form of woman
> All that is insupportable in thee
> Of light and love and immortality!
>
> Epips. 21-24

In fact, face to face with the glorious presence of his beloved, his only adequate reaction is silent awe in which he is only able to stumble about:

> Thou Wonder, and thou Beauty, and thou Terror!
>
> Epips. 29[72]

This reaction resembles closely a person's behaviour facing the revealed deity. Though some undefinable kind of terror befalls the viewer, he is at the same time fascinated by the beauty and filled with inexpressible wonder.[73]

---

[72]Cf. Song of Songs 6, 4: "Thou art beautiful, O my love, as Tirzah, comely as Jerusalem, terrible as an army with banners." - quoted from Wasserman, *Shelley* 421.

[73]Cf. Solve, Melvin T.: *Shelley. His Theory of Poetry.* New York 1964, p. 177: "Shelley usually makes no distinction between the beautiful and the sublime", and. "Everything is beautiful which in a greater or lesser degree participates in the universal idea beauty." - *ibid.* p. 178.

Nevertheless, the loved woman is not the unknown deity or spirit itself, but only an image of it, and 'shadow' is the most frequently applied term in rendering this concept.[74]

> An image of some bright Eternity;
> A shadow of some golden dream
>
> Epips. 115-16

Emily is an "embodied Ray / Of the great Brightness" (Fr. Epips. 38-39), "the shade / Of some sublimer spirit" (Fr. Epips. 43-44).

In "The Revolt of Islam", too, the same idea manifests itself in Cythna, who is,

> Like the bright shade of some immortal dream
> Which walks, when tempest steps, the wave of life's
> dark stream.
>
> C.II.XXIII.872-73

There is here, connected with the shadow-image - as in the context of the 'psyche - epipsyche' concept - the image of the mirror which reflects rays of light upon its surface.

Emily is not the light itself, but "a tender / Reflection of the eternal Moon of Love" (Epips. 118). Thus, the beloved is neither "some bright Eternity", nor "the great Brightness"; not "some sublimer spirit", not "some immortal dream", and also not "the eternal Moon of Love". But by being the image of them, she is an incarnation, an embodiment of the greater and brighter light indicated.[75]

---

[74] Cf. Spurgeon, *Symbole* 430: "Aux yeux de Shelley, ombre ne veut pas nécessairement dire absence de lumière, mais simplement diminuition de lumière."; for Shelley's use of shadows see Hawk, Susan Lee: *Shelley's Shadows: Studies in Analogy:* DA 31 (1971) 6610A.

[75] Cf. Kroese, *Beauty* 82: "Shelley is, right from the start, quite clear about Emily's image status. Apart from what she represents, Emily is of little concern in Epipsychidion."; similar Butter, *Idols* 33f.: "What was important to him was what was mirrored in them (i.e. the objects of his love) rather than the mirrors themselves."; Wasserman, *Shelley* 425: "a transcendent perfection

Shelley calls this glorious spirit, of which any earthly
beauty is but a feeble though transcendent shadow, 'Intellectual
Beauty', which also appears under the names of 'Spirit of Love'
and 'Spirit of Beauty'; they are identical and can therefore be
used interchangeably. Beauty and Love are - according to Shelley
- "but two modes or attributes of harmony, the underlying principle
of the universe, that which binds the world together."[76]

Shelley defines this Beauty as 'intellectual' to denote that
it is spiritual and "cannot be apprehended by the senses but which
paradoxically seems to flicker, sometimes just perceptibly, in a
whole series of natural signatures."[77]

---

[75] (cont'd) present in an earthly ambience."; Ebbinghaus, *Ein-heit* 74: "Einheit von transzendentaler Idee und personhafter Darstellung".

[76] Solve, *Theory* 169; "Love is a result of beholding beauty, and beauty is also produced by love." - *ibid.* p. 171; cf. Stovall, Floyd: "Shelley's Doctrine of Love": *PMLA* 45 (1930) 283-303, p. 297: "Intellectual Beauty ... is but a variant term for the Spirit of Love".; cf. Ebbinghaus, *Einheit* 83: "Die verschiedenen Benennungen der 'intellectual beauty' scheinen die Zuständlichkeit dieser höchsten Macht besonders stark zu betonen. Wenn dann aber zum Schluß der Hymnus (i.e. "Hymn to Intellectual Beauty") ausklingt in ein Bekenntnis zu der in der Menschheit wirkenden Liebe, so ist damit das Wesen dieser höchsten Macht eben als unvergängliche ewige 'love' charakterisiert."; in Canto I of "The Revolt of Islam" the Woman loved the Morning Star, Hesperus, or Venus, which was one symbol for the Spirit of Beauty in Shelley's poetry up to "The Triumph of Life" - see Lea, F. A.: *Shelley and the Romantic Revolution.* London 1945, p. 75f.; she further holds the opinion that, "the difference between his (i.e. Shelley's) One and Plato's is the difference of two thousand years of Christianity: Shelley's is supereminently a spirit of absolute Love. It is, therefore, indistinguishable from the Christian God, as he was, despite his superficial atheism, perfectly aware." - *ibid.* p. 80.

[77] Bloom, *Mythmaking* 37; for the genesis of this term see Rogers, who does not consider it Platonic - there is a "great fundamental difference between the Shelleyan lover and the Platonic one. It is that whereas the former is constantly seeking on this earth

This spirit of 'Intellectual Beauty', whom Shelley conceives as a personal Thou[78], manifests itself in earthly forms and lives within mortal frames.

> *Spirit of Beauty, that dost consecrate*
> *With thine own hues all thou dost shine upon*
> *Of human thought or form, -*
> Intell. Beauty, II.13-15

> *By Heaven and Earth, from all whose shapes thou flowest,*
> *Neither to be contained, delayed, nor hidden;*
> *Making divine the loftiest and the lowest*
> *When for a moment thou art not forbidden*
> *To live within the life which thou bestowest.*
> Zucca, IV.25-29

It may be present not only in inanimate objects of nature, like winds, trees, streams, flowers, leaves, grass, music, or voices (cf. Zucca, V.33-36.38), but also and pre-eminently in "the soft motions and rare smile of women" (Zucca, V.37). Its presence is always only a temporary one, which may be gone soon after its appearance.[79] It is therefore associated with the shadow, which is characterized by its evanescence.

> *The awful shadow of some unseen Power*

---

[77] (cont'd) for the shadow of an abstract eternal Beauty, the latter starts with the shadow of the earthly Beauty and immediately transcends it in a dialectical pursuit of its shadows in morals and sciences." - Rogers, *Shelley* 41.

[78] According to the great Jewish theologian Martin Buber, every It may become a Thou by entering into a relationship - see Bloom, *Mythmaking* 3; for Bloom's rendering of Buber's concept of 'I and Thou' see *ibid.* pp. 1-3; the revelation of 'Intellectual Beauty' to Shelley is described like a religious experience - cf. "Hymn to Intellectual Beauty", V.59-60; and Revolt, Ded., IV.27; see further Des Pres, Terrence George: *Visionary Experience in the Poems of Shelley:* DA 33 (1973) 6905A-6A.

[79] Cf. Mortenson, Peter: "Image and Structure in Shelley's Lyrics": *Studies in Romanticism* 4 (1964/65) 104-110, p. 117: "beauty is evanescent and comes by grace."

Floats though unseen among us, - *visiting*
This various world with an *inconstant* wing,
As *summer winds* that creep from *flower to flower*, -
Like moonbeams that behind some piny shower,
It visits with *inconstant* glance
Each human *heart and countenance*.

Intell. Beauty, I.1-7
(underlining mine)

And what *is* that most *brief* and *bright* delight
Which *rushes* through the touch and through the *sight*,
And *stands before* the *spirit's* inmost throne,
A naked Seraph! None hath ever known.
Its *birth is* darkness, and *its* growth desire;
Untameable and *fleet* and *fierce* as *fire*,
Not to be touched but to be *felt* alone,
It fills the world with glory - *and is gone*.[80]

Fr. Epips. 142-49
(underlining mine)

From this aspect it becomes clear why Shelley liked to define his
women - the incarnations of 'Intellectual Beauty' - as shadows, and
why he lets them act in the same fluent way.[81]

this glorious One
Floated into the cavern where I lay.

Epips. 337
(underlining mine)

But it is not only their floating nature which makes it difficult
for a mortal to behold them; this is also caused by their radiated
glory which - though only the shadow of the original - is still too

---

[80]Cf. Matthews, G. M.: *Shelley* (= *Writers and their Work* 214)
London 1970, p. 6: "What fascinated Shelley was not being but
process."; cf. Keith, *Imagery* 61: "Shelley's numerous images from
shadows, vapours, and clouds suggest that the ultimate meaning was
as uncertain to him as those unsubstantial elements. Consistency
he seems to have scorned."; this opinion is opposed to Carey,
Shelley 80: "it is because he was convinced that there was an ultimate meaning that he is so fascinated by the most shifting and
evanescent manifestations."

[81]For the influence of Spenser concerning emanation see
Maurer, *Frauen* 96.

bright for mortal eyes.

When the poet in "Epipsychidion" envisions Emily she is,

> *robed in such exceeding glory,*
> *That I beheld her not.*
>
> Epips. 199-200

And Emily is,

> *Scarce visible from extreme loveliness.*
>
> Epips. 104

To make her sight endurable, she is shrouded by a veil, which - although establishing separation - may be removed easily. Like the shadow-image it arises from Shelley's dynamic concept of life.[82]

Emily is the "veiled Glory" (Epips. 26) and is,

> *Veiling beneath that radiant form of Woman*
> *All that is insupportable ...*
> *Of light and love and immortality.*
>
> Epips. 22-24

Cythna's brightness, too, is hidden beneath a veil,

> *from that fair sight*
> *I turned in sickness, for a veil shrouded her countenance*
> *bright*
>
> Revolt, C.V.XLIV.2114-15

Thus, Laon remarks, and he hesitates - though it could be managed easily - to uplift this veil[83], conscious that the underlying glory would be too splendid for his mortal eyes.

In Shelley's work the veil-image is used in an increasingly

---

[82] Cf. Freydorf, *Bildhafte Sprache* 74; see also Fogle, *Imagery* 56: "Shelley's scientific bent also helps to account for ... his love of change, movement, and development."; according to Butter, *Idols* 97, many of Shelley's favourite images, among them 'shadow' and 'veil', are taken from Plato or are neo-Platonic; for the influence of Shelley's reading Wieland, Spenser, and Platonism see Rogers, *Shelley* 120f.; 'mist', 'vapour', 'cloud', etc. also belong to this category of Shelley's dynamic images.

[83] Cf. C.V.XLVI.2127: "Scarce did I wish her veil to be uplifted".

symbolic, intellectual sense, and first takes a more philosophical
colouring in later years.[84]

In "The Revolt of Islam", the veil is once mentioned as "the
mighty veil / Which doth divide the living and the dead" (C.XII.XV.
4581-82).[85]

In the sonnet of 1818, "Lift not the painted veil", life is
identified with the veil:

> *Lift not the painted veil which those who live*
> *Call life: Though unreal shapes be pictured there,*
> . . . .
> *I knew one who had lifted it - he sought*
> *For his lost heart was tender, things to love,*
> *But found them not, alas!*
> . . . . *a Spirit that strove*
> *For truth, and like the Preacher found it not.*
> ll. 1-2.7-9.13-14

In this case, the veil divides the empirical reality from the true
reality, the realm of the ideas.[86] The veil, thus, holds an intermediate place between divine and mortal.

An allusion to the ideal women's place in the universe may be
seen. They, too, stand between those two spheres. They belong
to the empirical world, but are an incarnation and manifestation of

---

[84]Cf. Butter, *Idols* 112 and Rogers, *Shelley* 121f.

[85]Cf. "Mont Blanc", 54: "the veil of life and death"; Butter,
Idols 111 raises the question whether this could mean "veil between
life and death".

[86]Cf. Keith, *Imagery* 63: "Shelley does not accept the visible
order as real"; Rogers comments that "a good deal of this Platonism
comes out" - Rogers, *Shelley* 122; "What the Veil comes to signify
here and throughout Shelley's mature work is the illusory world of
impermanence that hides of half the ideal world of reality." -
ibid. p. 123; for a parallelization of Shelley's veil and Plato's,
see *ibid.* p. 143: unreal shapes - εἴδωλα (Symp.), εὐκόνας, φάσματα
(Phaedr.); mimicked, as with colours idly spread - ἀνάπλεων σαρκῶν τε
ἀνθρωπίνων νων καὶ χρωμάτων καὶ ἄλλης πολλῆς φλυαρίας θνητῆς (Symp.).

the sublime.   Defined as 'shadows', they have the same function
as the veil has in the last quoted sonnet.   Yet here the emphasis
is not laid on the separation, but on their function as mediator.[87]

---

[87]"The figure of a female mediator between the realms of the
divine and the earthly is not new in Shelley's poetry, but the in-
crease in his need for what this figure represents is evident in
the ending of the poem (i.e. "Epips."), where he expresses in the
imagery of elopement his wish to merge himself with the One." -
Richards, George D.: "Shelley's Urn of Bitter Prophecy": *KSJ* 21/
22 (1972/73) 112-125, p. 122; this veil between false and true
reality may be lifted by "an identification with the beautiful
which exists in thought, action, or person, not our own." - Clark,
Prose 282; for the five different meanings of 'veil' in Shelley's
poetry, see Freydorf, *Bildhafte Sprache* 72ff.

3. "A METAPHOR OF SPRING AND YOUTH AND MORNING"
   (Epips. 120)

The change of time and the sequence of seasons played an important role in Shelley's concept of history and human life, which
he considered under the aspects of death and birth, decay and
renewal.[88]

> The blasts of Autumn drive the wingèd seeds
>   Over the earth, - next come the snows and rain,
> And frosts, and storms, which dreary Winter leads,
>   Out of his Scythian cave, a savage train;
>   Behold! Spring sweeps over the world again,
> Shedding soft dews from her etheral wings;
>   Flowers on the mountains, fruits over the plain,
>   And music on the waves and woods she flings
> And love on all that lives, and calm on lifeless things.
>   Revolt, C.IX.XXI.3649-57

Though manifesting a cyclical point of view[89], Shelley placed emphasis upon the new birth and renewal which recur but which tend to the
realization of an eternal Morning and an eternal Spring.

> Earth and Heaven
> The Ocean and the Sun, the Clouds their daughters,
>   Winter and Spring, and Morn and Noon, and Even,
>   All that we are or know, is darkly driven
> Towards one gulf.
>   C.IX.XXXV.3776-80
>
> 'This is the winter of the world; - and here
>   We die, even as the winds of Autumn fade,
> Expiring in the frore and foggy air. -

---

[88]Cf. Rogers, *Shelley* 26: upon Shelley "the seasons cast not
only a physical but an intellectual and moral influence which
practically became a feeling."

[89]As an image of the seasonal cycle, Shelley employed the
uroboros, the circular serpent, which became a central symbol of
change in his works, see Hartley, Robert Arnold: *Images of Change
in The Revolt of Islam:* DA 32 (1972) 3304A.

> *Behold! Spring comes, though we must pass, who made*
> *The promise of its birth, - even as the shade*
> *Which from our death, as from a mountain flings*
> *The future, a broad sunrise; thus arrayed*
> *As with the plumes of overshadowing wings*
> *From its dark gulf of chains, Earth like an eagle springs.*
> C.IX.XXV.3685-93

After snow, frost, and storms, spring brings about warmth and calm.
Its dews are soft, its wind ethereal, and it endows the world with
flowers, fruits, calm - and love. It will be noticed that these
elements are conceived as belonging together and appear but as different modes in which spring manifests itself, and in which its
presence can therefore be experienced.

As with 'Intellectual Beauty', Shelley conceived of spring as
a personal Thou, attributing it to the female sex. Spring, therefore, no longer remains only a season of the year, but it is also
the Spirit which brings new life to nature and love to mankind. Indeed, both love and life appear as synonyms in Shelley's poetry and
may be used interchangeably.

In "The Revolt of Islam", Shelley addresses Spring as a personal counterpart whom he considers to be the emblem of love. Thus,
what Spring is to world and nature, love is to man. The main function of both is revival:

> *'O Spring, of hope, and love, and youth, and gladness*
> *Wind-wingèd emblem! brightest, best and fairest!*
> *Whence comest thou, when, with dark Winter's sadness*
> *The tears that fade in sunny smiles thou sharest?*
> *Sister of joy, thou art the child who wearest*
> *Thy mother's dying smile, tender and sweet;*
> *Thy mother Autumn, for whose grave thou bearest*
> *Fresh flowers, and beams like flowers, with gentle feet,*
> *Disturbing not the leaves which are her winding sheet.*
> C.IX.XXII.3658-66

In this passage, as elsewhere in Shelley's poetry, Autumn is considered the mother of Spring. The traditional way of setting Spring
and Autumn, Summer and Winter into contrast is no longer maintained

in Shelley's concept; for him, Winter is the true contrast to
Spring. This follows exactly Shelley's cyclical view of time, in
which Winter is replaced by Spring, and the change from Winter to
Spring is the clashing of opposites in which the latter proves itself stronger.

This concept of nature was so dominant in Shelley's thought
that it also found entrance into his idea of women. After having
realized how Shelley associated his female ideals - in poetry and
life - with light and all its positive qualities, the idea of an
allusion between those incarnations of glory and brightness and
spring as well as morning offered itself to the poet. What day is
to night and spring to winter, the woman is to her lover:

> She met me, Stranger, upon life's rough way,
> And lured me towards sweet Death; as Night by Day,
> Winter by Spring, or sorrow by swift Hope,
> Led into light, life, peace.
> Epips. 72-75

She is the "Radiant Sister of the Day" (Jane, Invit. 47). When
she - like "an Incarnation of the Sun" (Epips. 335) - enters the
darkness of the world, a new day springs forth which enlightens and
refreshes what has lain barren and obscure. Her appearance
resembles the rising sun which brings about dawn and a new day:
Cythna is "calm, radiant, like the phantom of the dawn, / A spirit
from the caves of daylight" (Revolt, C.XII.XIII.420-21), and "her
lightness" is "Most like some radiant cloud of morning dew" (C.II.
XXIII.867-68); The presence of Emily means the dawn for her poet-
lover's long and unendurable night:

> and in her beauty's glow
> I stood, and felt the dawn of my long night.
> Epips. 340-41[90]

---

[90]Cf. Fr. Epips. 404-7:
"Love itself has power to change - ...
For it can burst his charnel, and make free

Even more frequently than the comparison of the change from night to day, Shelley applied his concept of seeing the beloved woman as an embodiment of and co-operator with spring.   Like spring itself, she enters into the winter of the world.   When the poet in "Epipsychidion" finally meets his long searched-for prototype, Emily appears in "splendour like the Morn's" (24) and radiates life:

> At length, into the obscure Forest came,
> The vision I had sought through grief and shame.
> Athwart that wintry wilderness of thorns
> Flashed from her motion splendour like the Morn's,
> And from her presence life was radiated
> Through the gray earth and branches bare and dead;
> So that harmony was paved, and roofed above
> With flowers as soft as thoughts of budding love.
>
> Epips. 321-28

And her glory is bright and powerful enough to revive what was dead and pierce the cold air with her "warm shade":

> The glory of her being, issuing thence,
> Stains the dead, blank, cold air with a warm shade
> Of unentangled intermixture, made
> By Love, of light and motion.
>
> Epips. 91-94[91]

In his life, Shelley himself could experience this revival brought about by the beloved woman.   In the Dedication to "The Revolt of Islam", he renders the effect which Mary had on him:

> Thou friend, whose presence on my wintry heart
> Fell, like bright spring upon some herbless plain.
>
> Revolt, Ded., VII.55

His heart, which had been frozen and barren, was melted and revived by his second wife.   While other hearts were but cold and icy

---

90 (cont'd) The limbs in chains, the heart in agony,
The soul in dust and chaos."

[91]Cf. "To Harriet" (1814) 8: "the warm sunshine of thine eyes"; Revolt, C.I.XVI.264-65: the Woman is "fair as one flower adorning an icy wilderness".

stones, Mary brought new life:

> *Hard hearts, and cold, like weights of icy stone*
> *Which crushed and withered mine, that could not be*
> *Aught but a lifeless clod, until revived by thee.*
> Revolt, Ded., VI.52-54

The centre of this reviving strength lies in the woman's heart, which is a paradise of everlasting spring:

> *turn thine eyes*
> *On thine own heart - it is a paradise*
> *Which everlasting Spring has made its own,*
> *And while drear Winter fills the naked skies,*
> *Sweet streams of sunny thought[92], and flowers fresh-blown,*
> *Are there, weave their sounds and odours into one.*
> Revolt, C.IX.XXVI.3697-702[93]

Even when surrounded by Winter's frost, the beloved remains un-affected, because,

> *time shall be forgiven,*
> *Though it changes all but thee.*
> C.IX.XXXV.3781-82

She is:

> *A well of sealed and secret happiness,*
> *Whose waters like blithe light and music are,*
> *Vanquishing dissonance and gloom.*
> Epips. 58-60[94]

As she is herself above all change, she can alter and transfigure the world surrounding her. Her waters are endowed with light and music. These two elements and flowers are the emblems of spring

-----

[92]Cf. Epips. 68: Emily is "A cradle of young thoughts of wingless pleasure".

[93]Cf. Revolt, C.VIII.XXII.3394-95:
"And love and joy can make the foulest breast
A paradise of flowers, where peace might build her nest."

[94]Consider the double meaning of the word 'spring', which can mean 'season' as well as 'fountain', 'well'; cf. Song of Songs 4, 12: the bride is "a spring shut up, a fountain sealed" - quoted from Wasserman, *Shelley* 421f.

in Shelley's concept.   Expressed in aural imagery, she vanquishes
dissonance in the realm of music and thus creates harmony;   the
same idea rendered in visual imagery is her functioning as light
piercing the gloom.[95]

In the same context, Shelley was fond of using flower-imagery
to denote the beloved's transfigurative power.   The poet of "Epipsychidion" suspends his words as "votive wreaths of withered
memory" (4).   They are inadequate means of mediation and but feeble
shadows of the original and genuine experience.[96]   The song which
the lover lays at the feet of his beloved is presented as the faded
blossom of a once fresh and lovely rose:

> *This song shall be thy rose: its petals pale*
> *Are dead, indeed, my adored Nightingale!*
> *But soft and fragrant is the faded blossom,*
> *And it has no thorn left to wound thy bosom.*
> Epips. 9-12[97]

Hardly any hope seems to be left that it might regain its original
beauty.   It has entered into the course of decay from which normally no way leads back.   Nevertheless, the poet's belief is so strong
that he can ask her,

> *I pray to thee that thou blot from this sad song*
> *All of its much mortality and wrong,*
> *With those clear drops, which start like sacred dew*
> *From the twin lights thy soul darkens through, .*

---

[95]Cf. Epips. 65-67: Emily is "A Lute . . . .
. . . . . to soothe the roughest
day
And lull fond grief asleep".

[96]Cf. Kroese, *Beauty* 85: "the fading of the poetic image is a
theme and a pattern within the poem".

[97]Cf. Leyda, *Eros* 56f.: "this rose, the symbol at once of
love and of the poem, differs drastically from the traditional
image ... The love described here begins - where most love poems
end and struggles throughout the poem to sustain the revival of
what he had abandoned all hope for, the resurrection, through Emily,
of the rose."

> *Weeping, till sorrow becomes ecstasy:*
> *Then smile on it, so that it may not die.*
> Epips. 35-40[98]

This passage hints at another quality of Emily - she appears trium-
phant also over mortality and consequently is an emblem of eternal
youth.   For her fight against any kind of decay she is equipped
with two weapons - her tears and her smile.   Her tears, "like
sacred dew", blot out and wash away all negative attributes -
whether it be wrongness, sorrow, or even mortality.   Once the
cleansing process is done with, her smile renews the barren and
empty land and fills it with new light which has the power to make
things grow.[99]   Tears and smile are both necessary, just as a flower
requires rain and sunshine to prosper, and it can be traced in Shelley's poetry that he liked to mention them together and thus made
clear that he considered them inseparable.[100]   As rain and sunshine

---

[98]This prayer sounds like an echo of Psalm 51:   "... according
unto the multitude of thy tender mercies blot out my transgressions.
Wash me throughly from mine iniquity, and cleanse me from my sin." -
quoted from Wasserman, *Shelley* 457;   cf. Ford, Newell F.:   "The
Symbolism of Shelley's Nightingales": *The Modern Language Review*
55 (1960) 569-574, p. 572:   "The poet is consciously reversing the
sexes of the Persian legend, in which the male nightingale sings to
the (female) rose until it blooms.";   'sacred dews' - "the traditional symbol of the divine grace given to man in his mortal state."
- Wasserman, *Shelley* 426.

[99]Cf. Magn. Lady, IV. 29-34:
"My soul weeps healing rain
On thee, thou withered flower!
It breathes mute music on thy sleep;
    Its odour calms thy brain!
Its light within thy gloomy breast
    Spreads like a second youth again."

[100]Cf. e.g. Revolt, Ded., XI.95-97:   "And in thy sweetest
smiles, and in thy tears, / And in thy gentle speech, a prophecy /
Is whispered, to subdue my fondest fears";   further, C.II.XXI.854-
55;   XXVII.909, etc.

are most likely to follow one another in April, the poet calls
Emily not only,

> A Metaphor of Spring and Youth and Morning[101]

but also

> A Vision like incarnate April, warning
> With smiles and tears, Frost the Anatomy
> Into his summer grave.
>
> Epips. 120-23

And if the lover views his beloved to stand "beside him like a
rainbow" (Revolt, C.V.XXIV.1929), the same images are implicit,
though now co-existent, the rainbow as the result of the sunshine's
reflection in rain-drops. Just as rain and sunshine descend from
the sky to nourish the earth, so tears and smiles have their common
origin in the woman's eyes. It can be noticed that Shelley -
throughout his poetry - attributes smiles more to the eyes, which
he conceived of as stars or the sun, than to the lips.[102] Lips,
in their turn, are frequently identified with flowers and ap-
preciated - like a flower's scent - for their odour and fragrance.[103]

> And from her lips, as from a hyacinth full
> Of honey-dew, a liquid murmur drops,
> Killing the sense with passion; sweet as stops
> Of planetary music heard in trance.
>
> Epips. 83-86[104]

---

[101]Cf. Wright, *Myth* 28: "indicates that she is herself a
metaphor expressively embodying for the poet's mind the relations
of spring to the year, youth to life, and morning to the day."

[102]Cf. Revolt, C.I.XXI.307-8: "Then she arised, and *smiled on
me with eyes* / Serene yet sorrowing, *like that planet fair*." (my
italics).

[103]Cf. Butter, *Idols* 73: "flowers were loved above all for
their scent"; Fogle, *Imagery* 85 states that Shelley's olfactory
images are generalized and light; this fact is proved by the sig-
nificantly frequent use of 'odour' and 'fragrance'.

[104]For this passage and line 105 cf. Song of Songs 4,11: "Thy
lips, O my spouse, drop as the honey comb: honey and milk are under
thy tongue; and the smell of thy garments is like the smell of
Lebanon." - quoted from Wasserman, *Shelley* 421.

> *Her marble brow and eager lips, like roses*
> *With their own fragrance pale, which Spring but half*
> *uncloses.*
>   Revolt, C.VI.XXXIII.2630-31

In another context, this fragrance is identified as love, with which
the lips fill the air they breathe:

> *her lips, whose motions gifted*
> *The air they breathed with love ...*
>   Revolt, C.IX.XXXVI.3786-87[105]

This odour may further be conceived of as resembling an invisible
flame:

> *Those warm and odorous lips might soon have shed*
> *On mine the fragrance and the invisible flame*
> *Which now the cold winds stole; -*
>   Revolt, C.XI.VI.4271-73

Besides attributing odour and fragrance to the beloved's lips, Shelley conceived of these attributes as being issued from her hair and
dress.

> *Warm fragrance seems to fall from her light dress*
> *And from her loose hair; and where some honey tress*
> *The air of her own speed has disentwined,*
> *The sweetness seems to satiate the faint wind;*
> *And in the soul a wild odour is felt,*
> *Beyond the sense, like fiery dews that melt*
> *Into the bosom of a frozen bud.*
>   Epips. 105-11

> *Within thy breath, and on thy hair, like odour, it is yet,*
> *And from thy touch like fire doth leap.*
>   Const. Sing., I.6-7

This odour either kills the senses or is felt beyond them, but it is
of such an extraordinary kind that senses are unable to behold it.

An outstanding combination created by Shelley comes in here.
Odour and fragrance function like light in dissolving the cold air
and melting the frozen bud:

---

[105]Cf. Magn. Lady, IV.31-32: Jane's soul "breathes mute
music on thy sleep; / Its odour calms thy brain!".

> *odours warm and fresh fell from her hair*
> *Dissolving the dull cold in the frore air.*
>
> Epips. 333-34

The flower-imagery and its implication for fading offered itself
quite readily to express mutability and transitoriness of beauty,
and especially of love. As such, it was applied in "On a Faded
Violet"[106], in which the beloved's kisses are compared to a withered
flower:

> *The odour from the flower is gone*
> *Which like thy kisses breathed on me;*
> *The colour from the flower is flown*
> *Which glowed of thee and only thee.*
>
> I. 1-4[107]

A variant of this idea is presented in the short poem "To -,
'Music, when soft voices die'".   In it, odour is conceived of as
what remains when the flower fades and thus is compared to memory
left when the beloved object is gone.

> *Odours, when sweet violets sicken,*
> *Live within the sense they quicken.*
>
> *Rose leaves, when the rose is dead,*
> *Are heaped for the beloved's bed,*
> *And so thy thoughts, when thou art gone,*
> *Love itself shall slumber on.*
>
> ll. 3-8

The implied association of flower and thought is a common one with
Shelley.[108]

---

[106]Violets were Shelley's favourite flowers, cf. Butter, *Idols* 73.

[107]Cf. "Remembrance", 1-4: The flower that smiles to-day /
To-morrow dies; / All that we wish to stay / Tempts and then flies."

[108]Cf. Epips. 328: "flowers as soft as thoughts"; Epips. 4:
"wreaths of withered memory"; Epips. 383-87:
> "Lady mine,
> Scorn not these flowers of thought, the fading birth
> Which from its heart of hearts that plant puts forth
> Whose fruit, made perfect by thy sunny eyes,
> Will be as of the trees of Paradise."

cf. also Revolt, C.IX.XXVI.3701: "Sweet streams of sunny thought,
and flowers fresh-blown".

Whereas in "Epipsychidion" the withered rose stands for the
song, it signifies the lover's mental state in another poem.   In
"To Constantia", Shelley describes the influence of Claire Claremont on him in terms of the rose under the influence of night and
day:

> The rose that drinks the fountain dew
>   In the pleasant air of noon,
> Grows pale and blue with altered hue -
>   In the gaze of the nightly moon;
> For the planet of frost, so cold and bright
> Makes it wan with her borrowed light.
>
> Such is my heart - roses are fair
>   And at best a withered blossom;
> But thy false care did idly wear
>   Its withered leaves in a faithless bosom;
> And fed like love, like air and dew,
> Its growth -
>
> I.II.

Whereas the "air of noon" makes the rose-heart flourish, it grows
pale under the influence of the "planet of frost", the moon.   Its
need is the genuine sunlight of the day, not borrowed light which
is a diminuition of the original.

CHAPTER II

"SWEET MELODIES OF MUSIC"

(Revolt, C.VII.XXXII.3114-15)

AURAL IMAGERY AND THE SIGNIFICANCE OF MUSIC

Shelley's universe was peopled with songs, and music filled
the air like ethereal winds enchanting a summer day. He seemed
to have been aware of music everywhere. Nature itself was to him
like an orchestra in which water, mountains, plants, and animals -
especially birds - each played their part.

In "With a Guitar, To Jane" the guitar - an instrument con-
structed by man - found its model in nature and imitated it in its
own way:

> For it had learned all harmonies
> Of the plains and of the skies,
> Of the forests and the mountains,
> And the many-voiced fountains;
> The clear echoes of the hills,
> The softest notes of falling rills,
> The melodies of birds and bees,
> The murmuring of the summer seas,
> And pattering rain, and breathing dew,
> And seldom-heard mysterious sound
> Which, driven on its diurnal round,
> As it floats through boundless day
> Our world enkindles on its way. -
> 11. 65-78

What wonder then that Shelley considered love and all its associated
aspects in an increasing degree in terms of music.[109] The voice of
Emily reveals itself to the poet-lover in the various sounds which
may be heard in nature:

---
[109]Cf. Fogle, *Imagery* 82: "Shelley's more agreeable auditory
images are numerous but less fully realized than his discordances."

> *Her voice came to me through the whispering woods,*
> *And from the fountains, and the odours deep*
> *Of flowers, which, like lips murmuring in their sleep*
> *Of the sweet kisses which had lulled them there,*
> *Breathed but of her to the anamoured air;*
> *And from the breezes whether low or loud,*
> *And from the rain of every passing cloud,*
> *And from the singing of the summer-birds,*
> *And from all sounds, all silence.*
> Epips. 201-12

Every tone and sound could become the bearer of a melody which was able to reach a person beyond conscious or intellectual apprehension. In this mode of perception even a woman's voice could turn out to be not ordinary language, but a melody, tones produced by some fair instrument.

So the Woman in Canto I of "The Revolt of Islam" is endowed with a "melodious voice" (C.I.XX.301) and,

> *She spoke in language whose strange melody*
> *Might not belong to earth. I heard, alone,*
> *What made its music more melodious be,*
> *The pity and the love of every tone.*
> *But to the Snake those accents sweet were known.*
> C.I.XIX.289-93

Echoed in the caverns opening to the sea, these accents,

> *... filled with silver sounds the overflowing air.* [110]
> C.I.XVIII.287

The melody of this voice appears as a paradox, combining two contrary qualities. It is both sweet and wild.[111]

> *Her voice was like the wildest, saddest tone,*
> *Yet sweet, of some loved voice heard long ago.*
> C.I.XXII.316-17

---

[110] Cf. C.VI.XLII.2704-5: "The tones of Cythna's voice like echoes were / Of those far murmuring streams".

[111] Cf. Fogle, *Imagery* 82: "His (i.e. Shelley's) music is sweet, but elemental and unindividualized; it is thin."

This same feature is valid for Cythna's voice, which fills

> ... *the shore and sky*
> *With her sweet accents - a wild melody!*
> C.II.XXVIII.913-14

And although "those impassioned songs" (C.II.XXIX.922) are,

> ... *as a mountain-stream which sweeps*
> *The withered leaves of Autumn to the lake,*
> C.V.LIII.2281-82[112]

they are "accents soft and sweet" (C.VII.II.2847)[113], which people
the universe with "sweet melodies of love" (C.VII.XXXII.314-15).

Mary's voice, too, is an instrument pouring forth accents
which are love:

> *Your sweet voice, like a bird,*
> *Singing love to its lone mate*
> *In the ivy bower disconsolate;*
> *Voice the sweetest ever heard!*
> To Mary -, 3-6

And whereas Claire's voice in "To Constantia, Singing"[114] is again
both "a tempest swift and strong" (IV.35), Sophia is associated with
wildness more than with sweetness.[115]

---

[112]Cf. C.VI.XX.2512-13: "... her musical pants, like the
sweet source / Of waters in the desert".

[113]Cf. C.XI.VI.4245: "her voice, tender and sweet".

[114]The accurate text of this poem is contained in the
Silsbee notebook at Harvard University, once owned by Claire
Clairmont, see Curran, Stuart: "Shelley's Emendations to the
Hymn to Intellectual Beauty": *English Language Notes* 7 (1970)
270-273, p. 270; see further Chernaik, Judith: "Shelley's 'To
Constantia'. A Contemporary Printing Examined": *TLS* Feb. 1969,
p. 140.

[115]About her personality, King-Hele comments that, "There
was nothing remarkable about Miss Stacey ... except that she
could sing well." King-Hele, *Thought* 234.

> *... the fainting soul is faintest*
> *When it hears thy harp's wild measure.*
> To Sophia (Miss Stacey) III.15-16[116]

Emily's voice, on the contrary, seems to be apprehended as sweet and
mild only.   None of the powerful energy present in the women's
voices in Shelley's earlier love poems appears to be left.   Emily,
this "poor captive bird", is the source of only sweet melodies.

> *Poor captive bird! who, from thy narrow cage*
> *Pourest such music, that it might assuage*
> *The ruggéd hearts of those who imprisoned thee,*
> *Were they not deaf to all sweet melody.*
> Epips. 5-8

Her voice is "sweet as stops / Of planetary music" (85-85), like
that of the starry spheres (cf. 87).   Its "cosmic implications"[117]
transcend its earthly location and indicate its divine source.   The
beloved's melodious voice, in fact, "might not belong to earth"
(Revolt, C.I.XIX.290);   it sounds "like a spirit's tongue" (C.II.
XXVIII.917), and is "like music of some minstrel heavenly-gifted"
(C.V.XLVI.2125).   In "To Jane, 'The Keen Stars Were Twinkling'",
the woman's voice is,

> A tone
> *Of some world far from ours,*
> *Where music and moonlight and feeling*
> *Are one.*
> IV.21-24

By her singing she can translate this far-away world which is
characterized by synaesthesia, a harmony of the senses, into the
present empirical world.[118]   Her song belongs to both spheres and

---

[116]Cf. Const. Sing., I.4-5:   "... the sounds which were thy
voice, which *burn* / Between thy lips..." (my italics).

[117]Kroese, *Beauty* 96.

[118]Mertens, Helmut: "Entsprechung von Form und Gehalt in
Shelley's Gedicht To Jane: "The Keen Stars Were Twinkling"": *Die
Neueren Sprachen* 1964, 229-233, p. 232 comments, "Als ein von den

can therefore function as a mediator.

This melody is associated with the wind; it even becomes the
air we breathe itself:

> In *tones whose sweetness silence did prolong,*
> *As if to lingering winds they did belong,*
> *Poured forth her inmost soul.*
> Revolt, C.V.LII.2275-77

> '*Thy songs were winds whereon I fled at will,*
> *As in a wingèd chariot.*
> C.VII.XXXIII.3118-19

Cythna's accents are also defined as odours floating in the air:

> ... *thine own wild songs which in the air*
> *Like homeless odours floated ...*
> C.IX.XII.3574-75

And Claire's voice is,

> ... *like the world-surrounding air, thy song*
> *Flows on, and fills all things with melody.-*
> Const. Sing., IV.33-34

It is to be noticed that music is never conceived as static, but
always as being in motion. As such it flows and floats - a charac-

---

118 (cont'd)Romantikern allgemein häufig angewandter Stilzug
besitzt die Synästhesia ihre innere Rechtfertigung in diesem Gedicht
in besonders hohem Maße. Denn hier geschieht auf der Ebene der
Form genau das, was auf der Ebene des Gehalts als höchstes Ideal des
dichterischen Verlangens gilt. So wie hier zwei Sinneseïndrücke
miteinander verschmolzen werden, so bilden in jener weit entfernten
Traumwelt, von der wir nur einen Abglanz erkennen können, die Dinge
eine geheimnisvolle Einheit."; for a detailed study of synaesthesia,
see Erhardt-Siebold, Erika von: "Harmony of the Senses in English,
German, and French Romanticism": *PMLA* 47 (1932) 577-592; she defines the term 'synaesthesia' as "that curious faculty of harmony
between the senses, whereby a given strong impulse not only causes
the sense actually stimulated to response, but compels other senses
to vibrate simultaneously." - *ibid.* p. 580f.; for the parallelism
between 'starlight - notes of the guitar', and 'moonlight - singing'
in the poem "To Jane, 'The Keen Stars Were Twinkling'", see further
Butter, *Idols* 38 and Wilson, *Later Poetry* 38.

teristic of the air, but also of water.[119]   Thus, the beloved's
voice is further identified with waves or her singing co-operates
with the sounds of the waves to compose a harmonious melody.
Cythna sings,

> *Triumphant strains, ... like a spirit's tongue*
> *To the enchanted waves ...*
> C.II.XXVIII.917-18[120]

The waves appear as the accompanying instrument to the human voice.
Thus, waves may function in the way Jane's guitar does in "To
Jane, 'The Keen Stars Were Twinkling'".   Both guitar and human
voice are meant for one another, because the latter gives the former
the soul which it lacks.

> *The guitar was tinkling,*
> *But the notes were not sweet till you sung them*
> *Again.*
>
> *So your voice most tender*
> *To the strings without soul had then given*
> *Its own.*
> I.4-6; II.10-12

The waves of music are pictured from still another point of view;
the notes represent a medium on which the poet or lover can float
like a boat on the waves of an ocean or stream:

> *My spirit like a charmèd bark doth swim*
> *Upon the liquid waves of thy sweet singing*
> *For far away into the regions dim*
>
> *Of rapture - as a boat, with swift sails winging*
> *Its way adown some many-winding river,*
> *Speeds through dark forests o'er the waters singing.*
> Fragment: To One Singing[121]

---

[119]Cf. Further Const. Sing., III.21-22: "Her voice is hover-
ing o'er my soul - it lingers / O'ershadowing it with soft and
lulling wings."

[120]Cf. C.XII.XX.4623: "the waves which sung".

[121]Cf. Prom. Unb. II.V.72-74:

Shelley also used to employ the wave-image identified with music to
render the effect mental impressions left behind on man's passive
soul:

> ... *on my passive soul there seemed to creep*
> *A melody, like waves in wrinkled sands that leap.*
> Revolt, C.XII.XVII.4601-2[122]

The effect of the beloved's singing is expressed in the same terms
of floating movement.   It is a voice which "flowed o'er my troubled
mind" (Revolt, C.V.XLV.2124) and sheds calmness (cf. LVII.2135),
Cythna's singing to her lute is a power,

> *Like winds that die in wastes - one moment mute*
> *The evil thoughts it made, which did his breast pollute.*
> C.VII.IV.2864-65

Its influence is not only a calming one; it is also a combatant
principle against the tyrant's lusty self-love and all kinds of evil
and decay.[123]

---

121 (cont'd)"My soul is an enchanted boat,
            Which, like a sleeping swan, doth float
            Upon the silver waves of thy sweet singing."
In "To Constantia, Singing", the woman's voice is a tempest in
which the poet floats,
            "Now is thy voice a tempest swift and strong,
      On which, like one in trance upborne,
            Secure o'er rocks and waves I sweep,
      Rejoicing like a cloud of morn."
                                    IV.35-38

122Cf. Sensit. Plant, I.103; for Shelley's concept of the
human mind, see the study of Reisner, Thomas A.: "Tabula Rasa:
Shelley's Metaphor of the Mind": *Ariel* 4/2 (1973) 90-102; Shelley
distinguished two categories of mental impressions: 1. the sensory
and fixed, modelled upon the analogue of the tabula rasa: chronicle,
register, book of account, etc., and 2. extrasensory and ephemeral,
expressed by the sand-wave-image, see esp. *ibid.* pp. 94-96; Shelley
relied on Locke's image of the tabula rasa but reshaped it to his
own needs.

123Cf. C.V.LIII.2281-82: "Her voice was as a mountain-
stream which sweeps / The withered leaves of Autumn to the lake".

Emily herself is,

> A *Lute, which those whom Love has taught to play*
> *Make music on, to soothe the roughest day*
> *And lull fond grief asleep.*
>
> Epips. 65-67

Even the savage winds subdue themselves to her power and tranquillity passes over the world:

> *And music from her respiration spread*
> *Like light, - all other sounds were penetrated*
> *By the small, still, sweet spirit of that sound*
> *So that the savage winds hung mute around;*
>
> Epips. 329-32

In terms of music, Emily's voice is apt to overcome dissonance and bring about harmony. She is,

> *A well ...*
> *Whose waters like ... music are,*
> *Vanquishing dissonance ...*
>
> Epips. 58-60

Once, Shelley defines the lovers themselves as notes of music which are - though different - without discord and dissonance and produce a melody of harmony to fill the air:

> *We - are we not formed, as notes of music are,*
> *For one another, though dissimilar;*
> *Such difference without discord, as can make*
> *Those sweetest sounds, in which all spirits shake*
> *As trembling leaves in a continuous air.*
>
> Epips. 142-46[124]

Gifted with all those positive qualities of tranquillization and harmonization, this voice of the beloved has the power to enchant and disenchant; it is even powerful enough to open heaven and provide a possibility for insight into it by mortals:

> *The cope of heaven seems rent and cloven*
> *By the enchantment of thy strain.*
>
> Const. Sing., II.14-15

---

[124]Cf. Kroese, *Beauty* 96: "... the harmony created by two voices discovers something universal of which the notes separately are but a part."

Cythna's voice is,

> *Like music of some minstrel heavenly-gifted,*
> *To one whom fiends enthral, this voice to me*
> Revolt, C.V.XLVI.2125-26

And the music of her,

> . . . . *own sweet spells*
> *Will disenchant the captives.*
> C.II.XLII.1040-41

Similarly, the beloved's fingers, which strike the strings of the instrument, accompanying her voice, can also appear supernaturally gifted:

> *The blood and life within those snowy fingers*
> *Teach witchcraft to the instrumental strings.*
> Const. Sing., III.23-24

In making use of instruments, Shelley preferred to stick to string instruments like harp, lyre, lute, or guitar. It seems that the way they function corresponds best to Shelley's concept. In fact, in his "Defence of Poetry", he defined man himself as such an instrument:

> Man is an instrument over which a series of external
> and internal impressions are driven, like the alter-
> nations of an ever-changing wind over an Aeolian
> lyre, which move it by their motion to ever-changing
> melody. But there is a principle within the human
> being, and perhaps within all sentient beings, which
> acts otherwise than the lyre, and produces not melody
> alone, but harmony, by an internal adjustment of the
> sounds or motions which excite them. It is as if
> the lyre could accomodate its chords to the motions
> of that which strikes them, in a determined propor-
> tion of sound, even as the musician can accomodate
> his voice to the sound of the lyre.[125]

The Aeolian lyre employed here, rendering his idea about man's mind and the influence of mental impressions upon it, was a preferred medium of the Romantics to express their variant of the theory of

[125]Clark, *Prose* 285f.

cognition.   By adopting it, Shelley wanted to find accomodation
between Locke's sensualism and the intuitionalism of Descartes and
Leibnitz, and thus to render his belief in the simultaneous partic-
ipation of both object and subject in the cognitive process.[126]
Applied to the relationship of lovers, the Aeolian lyre illustrates
the process of harmony between them.[127]   The influence of the wind
on the lyre resembles that of the woman on her lover; both belong
together and function complementarily.   Love itself is conceived
as a wind which blows,

> ... o'er the wires
> Of the soul's giant harp.
> Fr. Epips. 137-38

The same concept of the Aeolian lyre also underlies the following
passage from the Dedication to "The Revolt of Islam":

> Is it that now my inexperienced fingers
>   But strike the prelude of a loftier strain?
> Or, must the lyre on which my spirit lingers
>   Soon pause in silence, ne'er to sound again.
> X.82-85

In the context of mutability, men may be,

> ... like forgotten lyres, whose dissonant strings
> Give various response to each varying blast,
> To whose frail frame no second motion brings

------

[126]Cf. Reisner, Metaphor 90; Erhardt-Siebold, Harmony 568
found out that, "For the first time in literature, with Madame de
Stael, the new music of romanticism, the Aeolian harp, is felt as
an embodiment of synaesthetic principles, as a combination of lux-
uries for the senses."; see also Curran, Emendations 272f.: the
Aeolian harp is a metaphor for poetic inspiration by Divine Power;
the act of the 'poein', the making of poetry, too, is developed
poetically through the image of the Aeolian harp, see Starling,
George M.: Shelley's Poetry of 1815-1816: Alastor, 'Hymn to Intellectual Beauty', and 'Mont Blanc': DA 29 (1968) 4506A-7A.

[127]Cf. Epips. 430-31: in their final island-home, "The blue
Aegean girds this chosen home, / With ever-changing sound".

One mood or one modulation like the last.
                    Mutability, 5-8

The same idea of the transitoriness of human life rendered
in terms of music is also present in "Lines: 'When the Lamp is
Shattered'".   The departure of love is made parallel to a broken
lute which no longer produces any tones:

When the lute is broken,
Sweet tones are remembered not;
When the lips have spoken,
Loved accents are soon forgot.

As music and splendour
Survive not the lamp and the lute,
The heart's echoes render
No song when the spirit is mute: -
No song but sad dirges,
Like the wind through a ruined cell.
                    I.5-8; II.9-14

In this poem, lute and lips - like the lamp - are looked at as con-
tainers whose contents flees when they are destroyed.   As the sweet
tones of the lute vanish, so do the loved accents - both are forgot-
ten and not remembered any longer.[128]

One characteristic and most notable feature of Shelley's aural
imagery is undoubtedly his "predilection for comparisons between
music and perfume, his favourite stimuli"[129].   Although common,
this combination was "more common in Shelley ... than in any other
poet - and ... especially associated with moments of love."[130]   The
origin of this synaesthesia is to be found in the already mentioned
Aeolian harp, which "was placed in flower-beds and flowered grottoes

---

[128]This concept differs from that in "To -, 'Music, when soft
voices die'", where the music vibrates in the memory even when the
voices are gone, see lines 1-2.

[129]Erhardt-Siebold, *Harmony* 591.

[130]Butter, *Idols* 73.

so that the wind brought simultaneously perfume and music."[131]
How Shelley apprehended music and odour simultaneously is explicitly
expressed in one of his letters when he described his sense-impres-
sions,

> ... with radiant flowers whose names I know not, &
> which scatter thro the air the divinest odour which
> as you recline under the shade of the ruin produces
> sensations of voluptuous faintness like the combina-
> tion of sweet music.[132]

This mode of apprehending reality is to be found in his love poetry,
too.   In Cythna's heart,

> *Sweet streams of sunny thought, and flowers fresh-blown*
> *Are there, and weave their sounds and odours into one.*
> Revolt, C.IX.XXVI.3670l-2

And of her songs the poet can say that,

> *... thine own wild songs which in the air*
> *Like homeless odours floated.*
> C.IX.XII.3574-75

Jane's soul in "The Magnetic Lady to her Patient" "breathes mute
music on thy sleep; / Its odour calms thy brain!" (IV. 31-32).

A passage from "Epipsychidion" bears the same significance.
In it the fragrance issued by Emily is compared to the music of the
spheres:

> *And from her lips, as from a hyacinth full*
> *Of honey-dew, a liquid murmur drops,*
> *Killing the sense with passion; sweet as stops*
> *Of planetary music heard in trance.*
> Epips. 83-86[133]

---

[131] Erhardt-Siebold, *Harmony* 586.

[132] Letter to Thomas Love Peacock, March 23, 1819; *Letters*
II.85.

[133] Cf. Sensit. Plant, I.25-28:
"And the hyacinth purple, and white and blue,
Which flung from its bells a sweet peal anew
Of music so delicate, soft, and intense,
It was felt like an odour within the sense."

Claire's voice, too, is felt like the scent of some lovely flower:

> *Even through the sounds which were thy voice, which burn*
> *Between thy lips, are laid to sleep;*
> *Within thy breath, and on thy hair, like odour it is yet.*
>
> Const. Sing., I.4-7

In the first example sounds and odours fuse into one another and create the impression of synaesthesia. If this complete identification is not achieved, the emphasis is placed either on one or the other of both elements.

As we can make out from the previously quoted passages, Shelley speaks of music's odour, the second being a quality of the first, or he makes them the components of a simile: 'music like odour' or he puts it the other way round: odour is felt as music.

Finally, a few words should be devoted to Shelley's view of birds and their function in music.[134] Although the "'shrill, keen joyance' of the skylark strikes Shelley's most characteristic note"[135], he preferred the nightingale and its sweet voice for use in his love poetry.[136]

> *... the lone nightingale*
> *Has answered me with her most soothing song,*
> *Out of her ivy bower.*
>
> Revolt, C.X.II.3803-5

---

[134]Cf. Butter, *Idols* 72: "The birds in Shelley, when not representative of greed or savagery or introduced to provide suitable décor for battle scenes ... are usually brought in for the sake of their song, they are voices rather than physical presences."; see further Ford, *Nightingales* 573f.: "They remain birds while they act as symbols."

[135]Fogle, *Imagery* 79f.

[136]Cf. what was stated above about the sweet and wild voice of Shelley's women; Ford, *Nightingales* 573: "The voice of the nightingale is, either in itself or by way of symbol, an epiphany of the Absolute ... it is a sign and assurance of the ultimate harmony and beauty. Its source is 'the burning fountain', the 'sustaining Love' that sweeps through this mundane fluctuant world so burdened by imperfection and sadness."

In "Epipsychidion" the poet calls Emily herself his "Poor
captive bird ... / ... my adored Nightingale!" (5.10).   Mary's
sweet voice, conceived as that of a bird, refers also to the nightingale - this is indicated by the "sweet voice", the "lone mate",
and the "ivy bower":

> ... *your sweet voice, like a bird*
> *Singing love to its lone mate*
> *In the ivy bower disconsolate;*
> *Voice the sweetest ever heard!*
> To Mary -, 3-6

CHAPTER III
"LOVE'S RARE UNIVERSE"
(Epips. 589)

1. IDEAL TRANSCENDENTAL REALMS FOR THE LOVERS
   (THE TEMPLE OF THE SPIRIT - THE LONE RUIN -
   THE ELYSIAN ISLE)

"L'anima amante si slancia fuori del creato, e si crea nell' infinito un Mondo tutto per essa, diverso assai da questo oscuro e pauroso baratro."

"The soul that loves is hurled forth from the created world and creates in the infinite a world for itself and for itself alone, most different from this present dark and dismal pit."

This sentence from Emilia Viviani's essay "On Love", with which Shelley introduced his "Epipsychidion"[137], corresponds to his own conviction that realms of love are to be different from the ordinary world, from a world which normally lacks love and is marked by the various aspects of deficiency and evil. To endure these empirical conditions and that which men usually call reality, love and the lovers themselves are forced to create realms of their own, realms which are transfigured by the unchangeable power of love and become microcosms and atoms of Eternity.[138] Their location is normally far away from the present world, in "Nature's remotest reign" (Revolt

---

[137]See Hutchinson, Thomas (ed.): *Shelley. Poetical Works.* A new edition, corrected by G. M. Matthews. London - Oxford - New York 1975, p. 411; translation by Rogers, *Shelley* 241.

[138]Cf. Eug. Hills, 1-4: "Many a green isle needs must be
                              In the deep sea of Misery,
                              Or the mariner, worn and wan
                              Never thus could voyage on."

C.I.XLVIII.553)[139], "where earth and heaven meet" (C.II.XXV.887).
They are in fact 'intermediate spaces', placed μεταξὺ θεοῦ τε καὶ
θνῆτου, between divine and mortal.[140]

In these realms in the obscure distance, the finite and infinite, the ideal and actual, the mortal and eternal, and Earth and
Heaven meet and are transfused into a harmony of different spheres.
Therefore, Shelley liked to identify these places with isles which -
by being surrounded by waves - are adequate images to denote some
kind of hidden mystery as well as solitude.

These realms were not only a part of his poetry but the strong
desire for remote places where he could find refuge and solitude and
a hide out together with his beloved formed an important aspect of
Shelley's life.[141]

As we know from his biographical dates and letters, he sought
solitude wherever possible, and due to his enthusiasm for boating,
this solitude was quite often sought on islands in rivers or in the
sea. Such favoured places were also the birth-place of a vast
number of his poetical works. "The Revolt of Islam", for example,
was mainly written floating in a boat on the river Thames[142], in a
kind of refuge among islands, water, bower, etc.:

---

[139]Cf. Const. Sing., II.19: "... the verge of Nature's utmost
sphere ...".

[140]This definition is taken from Plato's "Symposium", see
Rogers, *Shelley* 56-61; such an ideal realm is the 'cope of heaven',
the ὑπερουράνιος τόπος of the "Phaedrus", the 'heaven above the
heavens', 'height of Love's rare universe'; the latter is also
Dante's 'Third Sphere', see Rogers, *Shelley* 97.142.246; cf. Salama,
Major Poems 234: according to Plato, the 'Third Heaven' or 'Sphere'
is the Heaven of Love and Rhetoric.

[141]Cf. Shelley's Italian verse fragment: "... far from all
pain I will chose a (   ) on the purple Ocean (heaven,) a quiet
refuge, which (   ) when (x - ", see Rogers, *Shelley* 242.

[142]Cf. the Notes by Mrs Shelley, Hutchinson, *Poetical Works*
156.

> *... where the woods to frame a bower*
> *With interlacēd branches mix and meet,*
> *Or where with sound like many voices sweet,*
> *Waterfalls leap among wild islands green,*
> *Which framed for my lone boat a lone retreat*
> *Of moss-green trees and weeds ...*
>
> Revolt, Ded., II.12-17

The images indicated in this passage are employed and further expanded in his poems. Though with slight changes here and there, Shelley's ideal realms share the same underlying concept and characteristics. It is surprising how the description of these realms in Shelley's poetry corresponds to a sketch he made in 1817.[143]

When in Canto I of "The Revolt of Islam" the Woman and the poet "had passed the ocean / Which girds the pole, Nature's remotest reign" (C.I.XLVIII.552-53), they enter into a fairy-like realm with

> *... a pellucid plain*
> *Of waters, azure with the noontide day.*
> *Ethereal mountains shone around - a Fane*
> *Stood in the midst, girt by green isles which lay*
> *On the sunny deep, resplendent far away.*
>
> C.I.XLVIII.554-58[144]

> *Winding among the lawny islands fair,*
> *Whose blosmy forests starred the shadowy deep,*
> *The wingless boat paused where an ivory stair*
> *Its fretwork in the crystal sea did steep,*
> *Encircling that vast Fane's aerial heap:*
> *We disembarked, and through a portal wide*
> *We passed - whose roof of moonstone carved, did keep*
> *A glimmering o'er the forms on every side,*
> *Sculptures like life and thought; immovable, deep-eyed.*
>
> C.LI.577-85

The Temple in the midst of this green island surrounded by azure

---

[143]This sketch is now in the Bodleian Library in Oxford.

[144]Cf. C.XII.XXXI.4725-26:
"His realm around a mighty Fane is spread,
Elysian islands bright and fortunate."

water is the Temple of the Spirit, which is the Spirit of Good,
Love, and Beauty.[145]   It is the transcendental place where a
mighty Senate dwells and to which the spirits of Laon and Cythna
return after their death.   This Temple is not part of the empirical world, but belongs to heaven, to the spheres, and access may
be gained either by death (as with Laon and Cythna), dream, or the
exploration of one's own mind.[146]

> *It was, a Temple, such as mortal hand*
> *Has never built, nor ecstasy, nor dream*
> *Reared in the cities of enchanted land:*
> *'Twas likest Heaven, ere yet day's purple stream*
> *Ebbs o'er the western forest, while the gleam*
> *Of the unrisen moon among the clouds*
> *Is gathering - when with many a golden beam*
> *The thronging constellations rush in crowds,*
> *Paving with fire the sky and the marmoreal floods.*
>   C.I.XLIX.559-67
>
> *Like what may be conceived of this vast dome,*
> *When from the depths which thought can seldom pierce*
> *Genius beholds it rise, his native home,*
> *Girt by the deserts of the Universe;*
> *Yet, nor in painting's light, of mightier verse,*

---

[145]Cf. Ruff, *Revolt* 37f.: the Temple is in part patterned on
Spenser's "Fairie Queene"; Rogers, *Shelley* 110 discovered a parallel in imagery between Canto I of "The Revolt of Islam" and Cole-
ridge's "Kubla Khan", 35-40:
      "The shadow of the dome of pleasure
      Floated midway on the waves;
      Where was heard the mingled measure
      From the fountains and the caves
   It was a miracle of rare device,
   A sunny pleasure-dome with caves of ice";
Rogers comments that, "Not only in the general imaginative conception but in verbal reflections of imagery the influence is a clear
one."

[146]Cf. Kroese, *Beauty* 64f.; he considers the Temple of the
Spirit to be the mind itself, the individual mind, but also the one
mind, of which the human mind is a part - see *ibid.* p. 61.

Or sculpture's marble language, can invest
That shape to mortal sense - such glooms immerse
That incommunicable sight, and rest
Upon the labouring brain and overburdened breast.
                                    C.I.L.568-76

In a next step the reader is introduced to the inside of the Temple.
It is,

.... a vast hall, whose glorious roof
Was diamond, which had drunk the lightning's sheen
In darkness, and now poured forth it through the woof
Of spell-invowen clouds hung there to screen
Its blinding splendour - through such veil was seen
That work of subtlest power, divine and rare;
Orb above orb, with starry shapes between,
And hornèd moons, and meteors strange and fair,
On night-black columns poised - one hollow hemisphere!
                                    C.I.III.586-94

This hall made of diamond receives and reflects light and by means
of phosphorescence[147] becomes a scene of great splendour, inhabited
by "starry Shapes", moons, and meteors. Even the "ten thousand
columns" (LIII.595) quiver light[148], and shadows, symbols for evil
themselves are turned to and become identified with light:

A shadow, which was light
                    C.XII.XVIII.4611

The Temple is further characterized by being furnished with
"Paintings, the poesy of mightiest thought" (C.I.LIII.600); and
music - which held a dominant role in Shelley's concept of the ideal

---

[147]This "is a Shelleyan image of the potential becoming
actual" - Hartley, Robert A.: "Phosphorescence in Canto I of 'The
Revolt of Islam'": *Notes and Queries* 20 (1973) 293-294, p. 294.

[148]Cf. Rogers, *Shelley* 116: "Eyes, Stars, Domes - all are
transfused in Shelley's imagery of Light: we see him playing with
them in his lyrics as with a box of translucent bricks. To his
more serious architectural constructions he already had, by 1817, a
full stockyard of these and other translucent, polychromatic mate-
rials - moonstone, saphire, jasper, meteors, moons, hollow half-
circles, and columns that mirror radiance. Out of these he built
a Temple, a 'vast dome' for Laon and Cythna."

realm - is presented by,

> ... *lyres whose strings were intertwined*
> *With pale and clinging flames, which ever there*
> *Waked faint yet thrilling sounds that pierced the crystal air.*
>
> C.I.LIV.610-12

When Laon and Cythna re-enter this ideal realm after their death, it is pictured in brightness and flower-imagery which is related to the moon and the stars. The odour of the flowers is even divine and the trees form a heaven:

> ... *Cythna sate reclined*
> *Beside me, on the waved and golden sand*
> *Of a clear pool, upon a bank o'ertwined*
> *With strange and star-bright flowers, which to the*
>   *mind*
> *Breathed divine odour; high above, was spread*
> *The emerald heaven of trees of unknown kind,*
> *Whose moonlike blooms and bright fruit overhead*
> *A shadow, which was light, upon the waters shed.*
>
> C.XII.XVIII.4604-11

In this Paradise (cf. C.XII.XXII.4643) the lovers experience "an eternal morning" (XXIX.4710), where they are forever "exempted now from mortal fear or pain" (XXIV.4665).

Unlike this postmortal realm, the old ruin of Canto VI, where Laon and Cythna consummate their passionate love after being re-united, is one of Shelley's transcendental realms placed amidst the empirical world and attainable within this mortal life. Its de-scription and location resembles partly that of the Temple of the Spirit, as it is girt by water and is a lonely place of retreat and refuge, too. This lovers' hide-out is,

> *A rocky hill which overhung the Ocean: -*
> *From that lone ruin, when the steed that panted*
> *Paused, might be heard the murmuring of the motion*
> *Of waters, as in spots for ever haunted*
> *By the choicest winds of Heaven, which are enchanted*
> *To music, by the wand of Solitude.*
>
> C.VI.XXIII.2533-38

Within that ruin, where a shattered portal
Looks to the eastern star, abandoned now
By man, to be the home of things immortal.
                    C.VI.XXVII.2569-71[149]

This place, looking to the eastern stars and enchanted by the murmuring waves and winds, has now become a realm of things immortal,
because it is ruled by eternal love: the union of the lovers takes
place under the control of 'Intellectual Beauty':

It is the shadow which does float unseen,
But not unfelt, o'er blind mortality
Whose divine darkness fled not, from that green
And lone recess, where lapped in peace did lie
Our linkèd frames ...
                    C.VI.XXXVII.2659-63

Like the Temple, the ruin has a hall, but a natural one made out of
weeds and leaves:

... a hall ... o'er whose roof
Fair clinging weeds with ivy pale did grow,
Clasping its gray rents with a verduous woof,
A hanging dome of leaves, a canopy moon-proof.
                    C.VI.XXVII.2574-77

Whereas the realm of the Spirit is characterized by immortality and
eternity, so in the mountain-retreat time is unfelt by the lovers.
As long as they stay there, united by love, the changes of time are
overcome by them:

... now
Had ages, such as make the moon and sun,
The seasons, and mankind their changes know
Left fear and time unfelt by us alone below.
                    C.VI.XXXV.2646-48

Another characteristic feature which marks Shelley's ideal realms is
also present here - as it was in the Temple. The lovers are wrap-
ped in sweet sounds of music spread forth by surrounding nature

---

[149]Cf. C.II.XXVI.894: "... the lone paths of our immortal
land ...".

which fills the air:

> ... the wintry loneliness
> Of those dead leaves, shedding their stars,
> The wandering wind her nurslings might caress;
> Whose intertwining fingers ever there
> Made music wild and soft that filled the listening air.
> C.VI.XXVIII.2582-86

> ... while the song
> Of blasts, in which its blue hair quivering bent,
> Strewed strangest sounds the moving leaves among:
> A wondrous light, the sound as of a spirit's tongue.
> C.VI.XXXII.2619-23

Undoubtedly one of the most beautiful illustrations of a
Shelleyan ideal realm is rendered in the third part of "Epipsychidion"
(lines 388-604), where the poet invites his beloved Emily to sail
with him to a lonely island where they can spend their days in
peaceful communion.   This island "under Ionian skies, / Beautiful
as a wreck of Paradise" (422-23) and surrounded by the "Elysian,
clear, and golden air" (427)[150] is of the same obscure and mysterious location as Shelley's other ideal realms.   Its place, too, is
somewhere between Heaven and Earth, on the far horizon of the
eternal ocean[151],

> It is an isle 'twixt Heaven, Air, Earth, and Sea,
> Cradled and hung in clear tranquillity;
> Bright as that wandering Eden Lucifer,
> Washed by the soft blue Ocean of young air.
> Epips. 457-60

Although in the world, this island nevertheless seems to be no part
of it.   It merely floats on an ocean which is also the sky and

---

[150]Cf. Revolt, C.VI.XXX.2603: "Beneath the golden stars of
the clear azure air".

[151]Cf. Rogers, *Shelley* 103: "Where it really lies, of course,
is somewhere in Plato's daemonic 'intermediate space', placed there
by Shelley and peopled and painted by him."

therefore is both an island and a star.[152]   Like the place of
refuge in the poem "To Jane, The Invitation", this chosen isle is
located,

> *Where the earth and ocean meet,*
> *And all things seem only one*
> *In the universal sun.*
>   ll. 67-69

"This chosen home" (Epips. 430) is indeed a "favoured place" (461),
which is deprived of evil and gifted with a wonderful calm and peace
amidst the storms of life:

> *It is a favoured place, Famine and Blight,*
> *Pestilence, War and Earthquake, never light*
> *Upon its mountain peaks; blind vultures, they*
> *Sail onward far upon their fatal way:*
> *The wingèd storms, chanting their thunder-psalm*
> *To other lands, leave azure chasms of calm*
> *Over this isle, or weep themselves in dew,*
> *From which its fields or woods ever-renew*
> *Their green and golden immortality.*
>   Epips. 461-69[153]

Like the Temple of the Spirit and the retreat-ruin of Laon and
Cythna, there is also a "lone dwelling" on this island.   It is a
building whose origin remains mysterious and whose architecture is
more Titanic than the work of human art:

> *But the chief marvel of the wilderness*
> *Is a lone dwelling, built by whom or how*   .

------

[152]"This border-status - an earthly island exhibiting the
characteristics of heaven - is manifest not only by its being like
the star of Venus, but also by its harmony with the air above, as
though the poet were at the same time describing a star under the
metaphor of a sea-girt island." - Wasserman, *Shelley* 442.

[153]Cf. Jane, Recoll. IV.46-48.52:
   "A thrilling, silent life, -
To momentary peace is lead
   Our mortal nature's strife;

   . . . .
   The lifeless atmosphere."

> *None of the rustic island-people knew:*
> *'Tis not a tower of strength, though with its height*
> *It overtops the woods; but for delight,*
> *Some wise and tender Ocean-King, ere crime*
> *Had been invented, in the world's young prime,*
> *Reared it, a wonder of that simple time,*
> *An envy of the isles, a pleasure-house*
> *Made sacred to his sister and his spouse.*
> *It scarce seems now a wreck of human art,*
> *But as it were Titanic.*
>
> Epips. 483-94

From the Advertisment to "Epipsychidion", we can see that this
"lone dwelling" was meant to be a ruin, similar to that in Canto VI
of "The Revolt of Islam":

> The Writer of the following lines died at Florence,
> as he was preparing for a voyage to one of the wildest
> Sporades, which he had bought, and where he had fitted
> up the ruins of an old building,..."[154]

Although Emily and the poet are not taken out of the course of
time, their lives on the island move on a different plane. Time is
no longer measured by clocks, but "the slow, silent night / Is
measured by the pants of their (i.e. the deer's) calm sleep" (534-35).

Nevertheless, the lovers are subject to decay and transitoriness, but the kind of death they will have to meet is nothing
frightening or associated with pain and sorrow.[155] It is merely a

---

[154]Hutchinson, *Poetical Works* 411; cf. Prom. Unb. III.III.22-
24: "A simple dwelling which shall be our own; / Where we will sit
and talk of time and change / As the world ebbs and flows, / our-
selves unchanged:"; cf. Wilson, *Later Poetry* 122: "Shelley's de-
scription of it (i.e. the ruined building) is perhaps his most successful attempt to present in poetry something of what he saw in
the ruins of Pompeii, Posidonia, and the Baths of Caracalla, here
transported to his pastoral Aegean isle."

[155]"The island represents the perfect condition of divinity
in the context of mutability and mortality." - Wasserman, *Shelley*
456; cf. *ibid.* p. 442: "... a perfectly ordered mutability as opposed to the chaotic contest of contraries"; "... life as a com-
promise between time and eternity" - Smith, Carolyn Wendel: *Time
and Eternity in Shelley's Major Poetry:* DA 33 (1973) 4364A.

continual fusion until the lovers become themselves the soul of
their isle; and thus, by replacing its present soul, they, too,
will become "An atom of th'Eternal" (179).[156]

> *Be this our home in life, and when years heap*
> *Their withered hours, like leaves, on our decay,*
> *Let us become the overhanging day,*
> *The living soul of this Elysian isle,*
> *Conscious, inseparable, one.*
>
> Epips. 536-40

> *And we will move possessing and possessed*
> *Wherever beauty on the earth's bare (?) breast*
> *Lies like the shadow of thy soul - till we*
> *Become one being with the world we see.*
>
> Fr. Epips. 183-86

This transfusion into the isle is also the striving towards identification of love and life, towards the full realization of a new and
harmonious universe:

> *Possessing and possessed by all that is*
> *Within that calm circumference of bliss,*
> *And by each other, till to love and live*
> *Be one.*
>
> Fr. Epips. 549-52[157]

---

[156]Cf. Notes by Mrs Shelley to "Prometheus Unbound", Hutchinson, *Poetical Works* 272: "Shelley loved to idealize the real - to
gift the mechanism of the material universe with a soul and a voice";
cf. Wasserman, *Shelley* 450: "That the island has a 'Soul' suggests
some version of the anima mundi, or demiurge, but that the island's
soul is an atom of th'Eternal, indicates a peculiarly Shelleyan attempt to relate the world to the transcendent."

[157]Cf. Prom. Unb. II.V.95-97:
"Realms where the air we breathe is love,
Which in the winds and in the waves move,
Harmonizing this earth with what we feel above."
Cf. Revolt, C.VIII.XII.3304: "To live, as if to love and live were
one"; C.IX.XXXVI.3788: "Fair star of love and life"; C.IX.XXX.
3730: "... our love and life..."; cf. Rosal. 622: "Love and life
in him were twins"; 764: "I loved, and I believed that life was
love"; cf. Epips. 345-46: "... this passive Earth, / This world of
love, this me"; cf. Wasserman, *Shelley* 456: "The most intimate

Until this state of complete fusion is reached, the lovers will
enjoy themselves in this azure isle-paradise with all its abundance
of flowers issuing forth lovely odours and blending with sweet
tones of music.   In all its beauty this ideal island is a regres-
sion to man's original state in the garden of Eden (cf. Epips. 417).[158]

> And all the place is peopled with sweet airs;
> The light clear element which the isle wears
> Is heavy with the scent of lemon-flowers,
> Which floats like mist laden with unseen showers,
> And falls upon the eyelids like faint sleep;
> And from the moss violets and jonquils peep,
> And dart their arrowy odour through the brain
> Till you might faint with that delicious pain.
> And every motion, odour, beam, and tone,
> With that deep music is in unison:
> Which is a soul within the soul - they seem
> Like echoes of an antenatal dream.
>   Epips. 445-56[159]

The simple life on the island "wants little, and true haste / Hires
not the pale drudge Luxury" (525-26).   But however simple and without materialistic needs it may be, it cannot be without music and
philosophy, which play an important role in the envisioned ideal
state, because they are able to establish a perpetual presence,
linking the future to the past:

---

[157] (cont'd) relationship they can attain in life is only the
mutuality of possessing and being possessed by each other and their
island circumference of bliss, while yet remaining distinct.";
Leyda, *Eros* 59: "The complete synthesis of the world of life and
the world of love is described in the imagined relationship of the
lovers".

[158] For the influence of the Italian landscape on Shelley's
picturing the isle, see Wilson, *Later Poetry* 102ff.

[159] Cf. Wilson, *Later Poetry* 232: "'Every motion, odour, beam,
and tone' is an echo of a world before birth into mortality, a
figure of pre-existence, to which the reminiscent 'soul within our
soul' responds, despite its burial in mortality."

> *I have sent books and music there, and all*
> *Those instruments with which high Spirits call*
> *The future from its cradle, and the past*
> *Out of its grave, and make the present last*
> *In thoughts and joys which sleep, but cannot die,*
> *Folded within their own eternity.*
>
> Epips. 519-24

By these two means eternity can be foreshadowed, because their qualities and beauty are everlasting.

Finally, in this total bliss of understanding and communion, even these two necessary requisites will be negotiated and a complete harmony in silence brought about:

> *And we will talk, until thought's melody*
> *Become too sweet for utterance, and it die*
> *In words, to live again in looks, which dart*
> *With thrilling tone into the voiceless heart,*
> *Harmonizing silence without a sound.*
>
> Epips. 560-64[160]

---

[160]Cf. Jane, Invit. 21-28:
"Away, away, from men and towns,
To the wild woods and the downs -
To the silent wilderness
Where the soul need not repress
Its music lest it should not find
An echo in another's mind,
While the touch of Nature's art
Harmonizes heart to heart."

2. THE LOVERS' UNION - "ONE SPIRIT WITHIN TWO FRAMES"
    (Epips. 573-74)

Amidst such a harmonious and enchanted landscape, secluded
from the dark sides of life, the lovers can enjoy and consummate
their cherished love.   In the lone ruin, Laon and Cythna can
celebrate their successful re-union and bridal-night in "A natural
couch of leaves in that recess, / Which seasons none disturbed"
(Revolt, C.VI.XXVIII.2579-80).   Their union comprises intellect
and spirit, as well as emotion and physical desire.[161]   This mingling of personalities is a loss of self, an oblivion, a fading
sleep into which the lovers faint and are dissolved:

> The beating of our veins one interval
> Made still;   and then I felt the blood that burned
> Within her frame, mingle with mine, and fall
> Around my heart like fire;   and over all
> A mist was spread, the sickness of a deep
> And speechless swoon of joy, as might befall
> Two disunited spirits when they leap
> In union from this earth's obscure and fading sleep.
>   Revolt, C.VI.XXXIV.2632-40

> Was it one moment that confounded thus
> All thought, all sense, all feeling, into one
> Unutterable power, which shielded us
> Even from our own cold looks, when we had gone
> Into a wide and wild oblivion
> Of tumult and of tenderness?
>   C.VI.XXXV.2641-46

The imagery applied to express the lovers' union sometimes takes on
the terminology of death.   Then, as in the case of Laon and Cythna,
it is a "failing heart in languishment", and "the quick dying gasps
/ Of the life meeting, when the faint eyes swim / Through tears of a

---

[161]For Shelley's view of erotic love and its significance, see
Brown Nathaniel Hapgood: *Shelley's Theory of Erotic Love:* DA 24
(1964) 4676.

wide mist boundless and dim" (C.VI.XXXVI.2651-54) express a kind of
dissolution and loss of control which the lovers undergo.[162]

A similar terminology and connotation is to be found in "Epipsychidion". When the poet meets Emily, the incarnation of his
vision and deliverance from his despair, she leads him into a kind
of death which is identified with life and in fact with true reality:

She met me, Stranger, upon life's rough way,
And lured me towards sweet Death;
Led into light, life, peace.

Epips. 72-73.75

Their envisioned union on the isle, expressed in sexual imagery, is

---

[162]Cf. Butter, *Idols* 19: Butter found in the above quoted
passages three main ideas: "(1) The lover becomes one in himself;
thought, feeling and sense are blent in one. (2) The lovers experience a dissolution, a kind of death, in which their souls are
united. (3) In this state, they are in contact with, or even part
of, a supernatural power."; according to Freydorf's division of the
three stages of ecstasy (state before, climax, and state after),
this stage of oblivion which resembles death belongs to the second
stage; see Freydorf, *Bildhafte Sprache* 18f.; "imagery of liebestod,
a passion culminating in death" - Richards, *Urn* 122; see further
Shealy, Ann Elizabeth: *The Shattered Lamp: A Study of Annihilation
in the Poetry of Shelley:* DA 33 (1973) 5141A; cf. Rosal. 1123:
"Heardst thou not, that those who die
Awake in a world of ecstasy?
That love, when limbs are interwoven,
And sleep, when the night of life is cloven
And thought, to the world's dim boundaries clinging,
And music, when one beloved is singing
Is death? ..."
cf. also the Fragment:
"I faint, I perish with my love! I grow
Frail as a cloud whose (splendour) pale
Under the evening's ever-changing glow:
I die like mist upon the gale,
And like a wave under the calm I fail."
cf. "The Indian Serenade", 17-18: "Oh lift me from the grass!
I die! I faint! I fail!"

closely related to the union of Laon and Cythna:

> *Our breath shall intermix, our bosoms bound,*
> *And our veins beat together; and our lips*
> *With other eloquence than words, eclipse*
> *The soul that burns between them, and the wells*
> *Which boil under our being's inmost cells,*
> *The fountain of our deepest life, shall be*
> *Confused in Passion's golden purity*
> *As mountain-springs under the morning sun.*
>
> Epips. 565-72

It is described in similar terms of mingling, fusion, and even dissolution and annihilation. Whether or not this illustrated union
is sexual, or only spiritual expressed in terms of physical union,
need not be our concern here, because whatever the decision may be,
the beauty of the passage remains unaffected.[163]

> *We shall become the same, we shall be one*
> *Spirit within two frames, oh! wherefore two?*
> *One passion in twin-hearts, which grows and grew*
> *Till like two meteors of expanding flame,*
> *Those spheres instinct with it become the same,*
> *Touch, mingle, are transfigured, ever still*
> *Burning, yet ever inconsumable;*
> . . . .

---

[163]Wilson believes that, "The ultimate union is apocalyptic
and cannot be contained in any earthly receptacle ... This world
must be scattered to the four winds and Time swallowed up in Eternity
before she and the poet can be transfigured." - Wilson, *Later Poetry*
233; see also Wasserman, *Shelley* 460: "What has happened is that
in the very act of describing the human interpossession of himself
and Emily in the world the poet exceeds the possible earthly limits
until, without his intending it, the mortal context has dropped out,
and he is actually describing the identity possible only in after-
life."; cf. Kroese, *Beauty* 82: "This sexual union is rather a metaphor of the spiritual."; vs. Fraser, *Shelley* 8: "The erotic climax
in Epipsychidion can, in fact, be taken as 'Italian Platonics' only
with a great deal of allegorical interpretation; it suggests far
more the glowing golden lust of Marlowe's Hero and Leander.";
similar, Leyda, *Eros* 56: "To explain away the physical aspect of
this union by calling it a symbolic image of spiritual passion is to
destroy the tension which the poem creates."

> *One hope within two wills, one will beneath*
> *Two overshadowing winds, one life, one death*
> *One Heaven, one Hell, one immortality,*
> *And one annihilation.*
>
> Epips. 573-79.84-87

This full realization of harmony between the lovers has its parallel in nature which corresponds to their unity:[164] It is, therefore, described in a similar sexual imagery, and in fact Shelley
"exploits all the physical trappings of the isle, which can be in-
vested with an erotic tinge."[165]

> *The mossy mountains, where the blue heavens bend*
> *With lightest winds, to touch their paramour;*
> *Or linger, where the pebble-paven shore,*
> *Under the quick, faint kisses of the sea*
> *Trembles and sparkles as with ecstasy. -*
>
> Epips. 54-58

> *And, day and night, aloof, from the high towers*
> *And terraces, the Earth and Ocean seem*
> *To sleep in one another's arms, and dream*
> *Of waves, flowers, clouds, woods, rocks, and all that we*
> *Read in their smiles, and call reality.*
>
> Epips. 508-12

The isle's beauty is compared to a bride who reveals herself slowly
by lifting veil after veil until the whole splendour of her naked-
ness is laid bare:

> *And from the sea there rise, and from the sky*
> *There fall, clear exhalations, soft and bright,*
> *Veil after veil, each hiding some delight,*
> *Which Sun or Moon or Zephyr draw aside,*
> *Till the isle's beauty, like a naked bride*
> *Glowing at once with love and loveliness,*
> *Blushes and trembles at its own excess.*
>
> Epips. 470-76

---

[164]Cf. Stovall, *Doctrine* 284: "Harmony of nature is evidence
of the presence of Love."

[165]King-Hele, *Thought* 283.

3. THE BOAT-VOYAGE

As Shelley's ideal realms are normally distant isles on a boundless ocean, they are the destiny of a dream-like voyage in a visionary boat.[166]   Shelley's boats are able to move from one sphere into another, from the empirical to the visionary, and from mortality into eternity.

As the boat is also a "common soul-vehicle"[167], the boat-voyage may also symbolize the soul's floating down the stream or ocean of life and mark changes in a person's mental state.[168]

The Woman's boat in Canto I of "The Revolt of Islam", in which she - together with the poet - makes her journey, is,

> A boat of rare device, which had no sail
>   But its own curvèd prow of thin moonstone,
> Wrought like a web of texture fine and frail,
>   To catch those gentlest winds which are not known
>   To breathe, but by the steady speed alone
> With which it cleaves the sparkling sea.
> Revolt, C.I.XXIII.325-30

It moves "swift as a cloud between the sea and sky" (XLII.544-45) in an 'intermediate sphere' between the waves of the ocean and the air above.   Its motion is characterized by a perpetual gaining of speed:

------

[166]Cf. Ruff, *Revolt* 40ff: Shelley was influenced by Thomas Moore's "The Grecian Girl's Dream of the Blessed Islands", especially by his concept of the journey over an ethereal ocean to an island; see further the study of Murray, Eugene Bernard: *Shelley's Use of the Journey Image:* DA 26 (1966) 4636.

[167]Butter, *Idols* 107.

[168]Cf. Zimansky, Curt Richard: *This Proper Paradise: A Study of Shelley's Symbolism and Mythology:* DA 33 (1972) 771A; cf. the parallel to Dante's sonnet to Cavalcanti, in which the idea of the soul-flight is symbolized by a voyage in a boat - see Rogers, *Shelley* 239f.

And swift and swifter grew the vessel's motion.
                                    C.I.XLVIII.550

The boat, in which Laon and Cythna return to the Temple of the
Spirit, resembles in construction that of the Woman:

> *The boat was one curved shell of hollow pearl,*
>   *Almost translucent with the light divine*
> *Of her within; the prow and stern did curl*
>   *Hornèd on high, like the young moon supine.*
>   C.XII.XXI.4630-33

And it, too, floats simultaneously on the water and in the air on
"sunlight's ebbing streams":

> *When o'er dim twilight mountains dark with pine,*
> *It floats upon the sunset's sea of beams,*
> *Whose golden waves in many a purple line*
> *Fade fast, till borne on sunlight's ebbing streams,*
> *Vilating on earth's verge the sunken meteor gleams.*
>   C.XII.XXXIII.4743-46

Like the Woman's boat, this boat of Laon and Cythna, guided by their
wingèd child[169], moves "fast and faster ... steadily speeding" (C.
XII.XXXVIII.4790-91; cf. XL.4802: "the aerial speed").

The boat in "Epipsychidion", in which the poet wants to go
with Emily to their "far Eden of the purple East" (417), is another
variant of Shelley's boats. It is defined as an albatross (416)
and thus the waters of the sea and the sky are again united.

Shelley's voyages, however obscure and mysterious they may be
and in whatever an uncertain sphere they may take place, always
reach their destiny and find their harbour, whether it is the ideal
isle,

------

[169]Cf. Ruff, *Revolt* 133: the image of the child as winged is
influenced by Plato's "Phaedrus", where the image of the winged
soul is used - the soul had wings before incarnation to show its
immortality and divinity; a person falling in love and admiring
the beauty of the beloved gains wings again; Cythna's child is the
fruit of her spiritual communion with Laon and her physical rape by
the Tyrant.

... Emily,
A ship is floating in the harbour now
Epips. 407-8

or the Temple of the Spirit:

And in the midst, afar, even like a sphere
Hung in one hollow sky, did there appear
The Temple of the Spirit; on the sound
Which issued thence, drawn nearer and more near,
Like the swift moon this glorious earth around,
The charmèd boat approached, and there its haven found.
Revolt, C.XII.XLI.4813-18

CONCLUSION

Only a limited number of Shelley's "thousand images of love-liness" could be dealt with in this investigation. Though they represent the most important and characteristic ones, there are still other minor ones left. Some of them were indicated when treating the main categories of Shelley's imagery.

In spite of the abundance and variety, Shelley's images are never discordant, but form together the unity of his poetical work. All of them manifest Shelley's habit of idealizing reality, which is indeed the most characteristic feature of his life and poetry and the outcome of the desperately searched-for eternity and its incarnations in mortal life. In a letter to John Gisborne, he once revealed his fundamental dilemma:

> I think one is always in love with something or other;
> the error, and I confess it is not easy for spirits
> cased in flesh and blood to avoid it, consists in seek-
> ing in a mortal image the likeness of what is perhaps
> eternal.[170]

And more than once after a love affair in which he was convinced he had found the incarnation of eternity in a woman he had to confess,

> I loved a being, an idea in my own mind which had no
> real existence.[171]

Although Shelley was never really willing to accept it, he became increasingly aware of the irreconcilability of the fundamentally different spheres of the eternal-divine and the mortal-human.

In the first preface to "Epipsychidion", which he later rejected, he commented about its presumed author:

---

[170] June 18, 1822; *Letters* II.976.

[171] To Hogg, June 2, 1811; *Letters* I.79.

He was an accomplished and amiable person but his error
was, θνητὸς ὤν μὴ θνητὰ φρονεῖν, - his fate is an additional proof that the tree of Knowledge is not the
tree of Life.[172]

"Being a mortal to aspire to immortal things"[173] was the most domi-

nant characteristic of Shelley which shaped his life until his

premature death.   And if we consider the epitaph attached to "The

Revolt of Islam", which is a quotation from Pindar's "Tenth Pythian

Ode", Shelley's innermost belief in the impossibility of reaching

the ideal realm within this mortal life becomes explicit:

But as for all the bright things that we, the mortal
race, attain he reaches the utmost limit of that
voyage.   Neither by ships nor by land can you find
the wondrous road to the trysting place of the
Hyperboreans.[174]

If not attainable within the limits of mortality, eternity and the

final realization of the ideal may be met beyond in a fundamentally

different life into which man enters after his death:

... *Die,*
If thou wouldst be with that which thou dost seek.
Adonais, 464-65

In this postmortal state, the lover's pains he had to suffer in

striving for an ideal relationship and counterpart will be rewarded:

'Love's very pain is sweet,
But its reward is in the world divine
Which, if not here, it builds beyond the grave.
Epips. 596-98

---

[172]Hutchinson, *Poetical Works* 425.

[173]This is the translation of the Greek phrase above by
Rogers, *Shelley* 75; Rogers supposes this phrase to be an adapta-
tion from Plato's "Timaeus."

[174]Translated by Rogers, *Shelley* 100.

LIST OF WORKS CITED

PRIMARY SOURCES

Hutchinson, Thomas (ed.): *Shelley. Poetical Works*. A new edition, corrected by G. M. Matthews. London - Oxford - New York ²1975 (= 1970).

Clark, David Lee (ed.): *Shelley's Prose. Or: The Trumpet of a Prophecy*. Albuquerque 1954.

Jones, Frederick L. (ed.): *The Letters of Percy Bysshe Shelley*. Vol. I.II. Oxford 1964.

ABBREVIATIONS

DA	Dissertation Abstracts
KSJ	Keats - Shelley Journal
PMLA	Publications of the Modern Language Association of America
TLS	Times Literary Supplement
Unpub. Doct. Diss.	Unpublished Doctoral Dissertation

SECONDARY SOURCES

Bloom, Harold: *Shelley's Mythmaking*. New York 1969.

Blunden, Edmund: *Shelley. A Life Story*. London 1948.

Brown, Nathaniel Hapgood: *Shelley's Theory of Erotic Love*. Unpub.
    Doct. Diss., Columbia University 1963 (= DA 24 (1964) 4676).

Brown, Richard Elwood: *Images of the Self in Shelley's Poetry*.
    Unpub. Doct. Diss., Cornell University 1972 (= DA 33 (1973)
    5165A).

Butter, Peter: *Shelley's Idols of the Cave*. Edinburgh 1954.

Cameron, Kenneth Neill: "The Planet - Tempest Passage in Epipsy-
    chidion": *PMLA* 63 (1948) 950-972.

Carey, Gillian: *Shelley* (= *Literature in Perspective*) London 1975.

Chernaik, Judith: "Shelley's "To Constantia". A Contemporary
    Printing Examined": *TLS* Feb. 1969, 140.

Curran, Stuart: "Shelley's Emendations to the Hymn to Intellectual
    Beauty": *English Language Notes* 7 (1970) 270-273.

Des Pres, Terrence George: *Visionary Experience in the Poems of
    Shelley*. Unpub. Doct. Diss., Washington University 1972
    (= DA 33 (1973) 5905A).

Ebbinghaus, Wilhelm: *Das Aesthetische Einheits- und Vollkommenheits-
    problem bei Shelley*. Marburg 1931.

Ellis, F. S.: *A Lexical Concordance to the Poetical Works of Percy
    Bysshe Shelley*. London 1892.

Enscoe, Gerald: *Eros and the Romantics. Sexual Love as a Theme in
    Coleridge, Shelley, and Keats*. The Hague 1967.

Erhardt-Siebold, Erika von: "Harmony of the Senses in English,
    German, and French Romanticism": *PMLA* 47 (1932) 577-592.

Evans, James C.: "Masks of the Poet: A Study of Self-Confrontation
    in Shelley's Poetry": *KSJ* 24 (1975) 70-89.

Fogle, Richard Harter: *The Imagery of Keats and Shelley. A Comparative Study*. Chapel Hill 1949.

Ford, Newell F.: "The Symbolism of Shelley's Nightingales": *Modern Language Review* 55 (1960) 569-574.

Fraser, G. S.: P. B. Shelley. *Adonais, Epipsychidion: Notes on Literature* 79 (1968).

Freydorf, Roswith von: *Die bildhafte Sprache in Shelley's Lyrik*. Quakenbrück 1935.

Furbank, Philip N.: *Reflections on the Word 'Image'*. London 1970.

Hartley, Robert Arnold: *Images of Change in The Revolt of Islam*. Unpub. Doct. Diss., Columbia University 1971 (= DA 33 (1972) 3304A).

Hartley, Robert Arnold: "Phosphorescence in Canto I of "The Revolt of Islam"": *Notes and Queries* 1973, 293-294.

Haswell, Richard H.: "Shelley's The Revolt of Islam. The Connexion of its Parts": *KSJ* 25 (1976) 81-102.

Hawk, Susan Lee: *Shelley's Shadows: Studies in Analogy*. Unpub. Doct. Diss., Yale University 1970 (= DA 31 (1971) 6610A).

Jones, Frederick L.: "Canto I of The Revolt of Islam": *KSJ* 9 (1960) 27-33.

Keach, William: "Reflexive Imagery in Shelley": *KSJ* 24 (1975) 49-69.

Keith, Arthur C.: "The Imagery of Shelley": *The South Atlantic Quarterly* 1924, 61-72.

King-Hele, Desmond: *Shelley. His Thought and Work*. London 1964.

Kroese, Irvin B.: *The Beauty and the Terror: Shelley's Visionary Women* (= *Romantic Reassessment* 23) Salzburg 1976.

Lea, F. A.: *Shelley and the Romantic Revolution*. London 1945.

Leyda, Seraphia D.: *"Love's Rare Universe": Eros in Shelley's Poetry* (= *Explorations of Literature* 18) Baton Rouge 1966, 43-69.

Leyda, Seraphia D.: *"The Serpent is Shut Out From Paradise": A Revaluation of Romantic Love in Shelley* (= *Romantic Reassessment* 4) Salzburg 1972.

Marshall, William H.: "Plato's Myth of Aristophanes and Shelley's Panthea": *Classical Journal* 55 (1960) 121-123.

Martinez, Alicia: *The Hero and Heroine of Shelley's The Revolt of Islam* (= *Romantic Reassessment* 63) Salzburg 1976.

Matthews, G. M.: *Shelley* (= *Writers and their Work* 214) London 1970.

Maurer, Otto: *Shelley und die Frauen* (= *Literaturhistorische Forschungen* 33) Berlin-Schöneberg 1906.

McNiece, Gerald: *Shelley and the Revolutionary Idea.* Cambridge - Massachusetts 1969.

Mertens, Helmut: "Entsprechung von Form und Gehalt in Shelley's Gedicht To Jane: The Keen Stars Were Twinkling": *Die Neueren Sprachen* 1964, 229-233.

Mortenson, Peter: "Image and Structure in Shelley's Longer Lyrics": *Studies in Romanticism* 4 (1965) 104-110.

Murray, Eugene Bernard: *Shelley's Use of the Journey Image.* Unpub. Doct. Diss., Columbia University 1965 (= DA 26 (1966) 4636).

Reisner, Thomas A.: "Tabula Rasa: Shelley's Metaphor of the Mind": *Ariel* 4/2 (1973) 90-102.

Richards, George D.: "Shelley's Urn of Bitter Prophecy": *KSJ* 21/22 (1972/73) 112-125.

Rogers, Neville: *Shelley at Work. A Critical Inquiry.* Oxford 1956.

Rosenfelt, Deborah Silverton: *Keats and Shelley: A Comparative Study of their Ideas about Poetic Language and some Patterns of Language Use in their Poetry.* Unpub. Doct. Diss., University of California, Los Angeles 1972 (= DA 33 (1973) 3669A).

Ruff, James Lynn: *Shelley's The Revolt of Islam* (= *Romantic Reassessment* 10) Salzburg 1972.

Salama, Adel: *Shelley's Major Poems. A Re-Interpretation*
(= *Romantic Reassessment* 9) Salzburg 1973.

Shealy, Ann Elizabeth: *"The Shattered Lamp": A Study of Annihilation in the Poetry of Shelley.* Unpub. Doct. Diss., Case
Western Reserve University 1972 (= DA 33 (1973) 5141A).

Slater, John Frederick: *Edward Garnett: The 'Splendid Advocate',
'Volpone', and 'Anthony and Cleopatra': The Play of Imagina-
tion, Self-Concealment and Self-Revelation in Shelley's
'Epipsychidion'.* Unpub. Doct. Diss., Rutgers University,
The State University of New Jersey 1971 (= DA 32 (1971)
3332A-3333A).

Smith, Carolyn Wendel: *Time and Eternity in Shelley's Major
Poetry.* Unpub. Doct. Diss., Brown University 1972 (= DA 33
(1973) 4364A).

Solve, Melvin T.: *Shelley. His Theory of Poetry.* New York 1964.

Spurgeon, Caroline F. E.: "De L'Emploi de Symbole dans la Poesie
de Shelley": *Revue Germanique* 8 (1912) 426-432.

Starling, George M.: *Shelley's Poetry of 1815-1816: Alastor,
'Hymn to Intellectual Beauty', and 'Mont Blanc'.* Unpub.
Doct. Diss., University of North Carolina at Chapel Hill 1968
(= DA 29 (1968) 4506A-7A).

Stempel, Daniel: "Shelley and the Ladder of Love": *KSJ* 15 (1966)
15-23.

Stovall, Floyd: "Shelley's Doctrine of Love": *PMLA* 45 (1930)
283-303.

Wasserman, Earl R.: *Shelley. A Critical Reading.* Baltimore -
London 1971.

Wilson, Milton: *Shelley's Later Poetry. A Study of His Prophetic
Imagination.* New York 1959.

Woodman, Ross G.: "Shelley's Changing Attitude to Plato": *Journal
of the History of Ideas* 31 (1960) 497-510.

Wright, John W.: *Shelley's Myth of Metaphor.* Athens - Georgia 1970.

Zimansky, Curt Richard: *This Proper Paradise: A Study of Shelley's Symbolism and Mythology*. Unpub. Doct. Diss., Indiana University 1972 (= DA 33 (1972) 771A).